P9-DCD-075

And Baby Makes More

And Baby Makes More

*Known Donors, Queer Parents, and
Our Unexpected Families*

Edited by
Susan Goldberg and Chloë Brushwood Rose

INSOMNIAC PRESS

Copyright © 2009 by Susan Goldberg and Chloë Brushwood Rose

All rights reserved. No part of this publication may be reproduced, stored in a retrieval system or transmitted, in any form or by any means, without the prior written permission of the publisher or, in case of photocopying or other reprographic copying, a license from Access Copyright, 1 Yonge Street, Suite 1900, Toronto, Ontario, Canada, M5E 1E5.

Library and Archives Canada Cataloguing in Publication

And baby makes more : known donors, queer parents, and our unexpected families / Susan Goldberg, Chloe Brushwood Rose, editors.

ISBN 978-1-897178-83-6

1. Lesbian mothers. 2. Lesbian mothers--Family relationships. 3. Human reproductive technology--Psychological aspects. 4. Pregnancy.
I. Goldberg, Susan, 1971- II. Brushwood Rose, Chloë T. (Chloë Tamar), 1972-

HQ75.53.A53 2009   306.874'308664   C2009-904623-7

The publisher gratefully acknowledges the support of the Department of Canadian Heritage through the Book Publishing Industry Development Program.

Printed and bound in Canada

Insomniac Press
520 Princess Ave.,
London, Ontario, Canada, N6B 2B8
www.insomniacpress.com

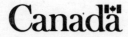

Table of Contents

Introduction

BY CHLOË BRUSHWOOD ROSE AND SUSAN GOLDBERG

In the beginning, it was all about the babies.

No, scratch that. In the beginning, it was all about getting pregnant. In the abstract, of course, it was about the babies, the children, the next 20-plus years. Many of us knew, in a visceral or a theoretical sort of way, that we wanted to have kids, wanted to be parents. Many of us were equally clear that we didn't want to raise children. But, for all of us, in the beginning, it really was about getting pregnant, about that science experiment of hopefully placing sperm in the proximity of egg and fingers crossed. And when — or perhaps even before — those two forces met and took on a life of their own, the reality hit: this was a Big Deal. This was serious. This involved *people's lives* — many, many people's lives. In ways that we hadn't really quite anticipated.

That's probably the case, give or take, for most expectant parents, for those of us who have to some degree or another wished for and planned, and then conceived and raised, children. For the queers among us, however, procreating has generally, and of necessity, tended to involve more lives, more decision-making, more intimacy, often more processing and imagining and negotiating and relationship-building than your average hetero coupling. If not more, than at least different. Unique. Perhaps unexpected.

The fact that there we're well into a "gayby boom" isn't news. The babies we have created are lovely, adorable, precious, geniuses, even well-adjusted, and so on — but on their own they are not the main story, at least, not for the purposes of this book. For the contributors to this collection, what is newsworthy are the families and friendships that these babies have helped to create and that have, mutually, created them. What is newsworthy is that these families gestate and shift and expand and accommodate and grow — and sometimes splinter apart — in ways that allow for, even insist upon, new ways of looking at what it means to be related to, responsible for, involved with, in love with, and chosen by the people around us.

And yet, the contributors to this collection consider the challenges and movements posed by their own families and relations while the ground continues to shift under our feet. This, of course, is one of the ironies of a collection such as this — the stories of our families are still being written, heard, told, while we attempt in some way to share in definitive terms what has happened to each of us. The continually shifting ground of family life demands an openness to the unknown, the unexpected, and — frankly — the ignorant, particularly for queer families who must contend with the "normal" challenges faced by any family while simultaneously pioneering new languages, laws, roles, and relationships.

Clearly, the creation of any child, to any set of parents — queer or not — is an inherently risky enterprise. It's just that, for queer families using known donors, that risk is often more visible. We vet potential donors or parenting partners, imagine endless "what-if" scenarios, sign contracts, involve lawyers, enter territory for which there is (often thankfully) no legal precedent. We deal — quite literally, sometimes — with the messy stuff, the most intimate versions of ourselves, and we often do it in public, under the scrutiny of our loved ones and our critics, and without much of a roadmap to go by. We create language where there was previously none, searching for the words, the terms, by which to define ourselves.

When prospective dyke mamas ask a man they know (or sometimes barely know) and trust to donate sperm; when gay dads-to-be watch a female friend give birth to their child; when a lesbian donates her eggs to her best straight pals; when a "single dyke" is vehemently not a "single mom" and a "sperm donor" is not a "donor dad"; when parenting dyads turn into triads and boundaries blur between "donor" and "lover"; when a trans mom donates her (carefully banked) sperm to her friends and her lover; when we are hit with infertility, miscarriage, paternity suits, custody battles, even hurt feelings — we take risks we never imagined and, in so doing, we create and name new ways of being "family," for better and for worse.

Perhaps this is the most important function of a collection like this: it offers us the space to name and describe these experiences of being ourselves and being family that are silenced by still all-pervasive ideals of the "nuclear family." And yet, the stories in this collection in many ways challenge the notion that the nuclear family has ever existed in isolation without a wider community, and they push us to reconsider our many family relations and experiences that are not governed by the strict codes of biology. While in many cases these are stories of finding (or not finding) the "right" — or at least readily available — biological stuff for baby-making, they are also stories that powerfully call on us to reconceive the family beyond biology.

While queer families often invoke the slogan "love makes a family," the stories in this collection insist on something else — love, yes, but also courage, patience, flexibility, generosity, and a sort of inclusion that can accommodate the unknown ways in which people may or may not come together to make a family.

We have been amazed at the diversity of roles that donors and parents — and their children — occupy, and the creativity and thoughtfulness they bring to those roles. Rather than asserting that their families are "just like everyone else's" (and, by extension, somehow, worthy of "equal" treatment or rights), the contributors to this book (mostly) revel in their families' uniqueness, see the unexpected as a strength, something to be celebrated, despite — or even because of — the challenges that difference poses. Because of this incredible diversity, and the shifts and risks inherent for queer families made through extended relations, we hope that this anthology provides, if not quite a complete roadmap, then at least an extended conversation and a place to begin to articulate a language that can work for ourselves and our children.

When the two of us first dreamed up this project, Susan had an eight-month-old son and Chloë was six months' pregnant with her first child. As we write this introduction, four years later, Susan's younger son is just about to turn two, and Chloë is a few days away from giving birth to her second child, who will be welcomed into the world by his three-and-a-half-year-old sister. The original impulse to co-edit an anthology on the phenomenon of the "known donor" reflected the realities of our lives: the intense, and in many ways unexpected, joys and challenges not only of conception, pregnancy, and early parenthood, but also of negotiating relationships with the men (ironically, both named Robert) who are our donors. Both of us, and our extended families, have been surprised, challenged, blessed, fascinated, and infinitely thrilled by the ways in which our risk-taking has been rewarded.

In the spirit of our continually shifting, evolving, and unexpected families, we look forward to the further conversations and future books this initial collection may incite. Our models for thinking about family and our language for telling our own stories are, at best, incomplete and, at worst, almost disabling. And yet the stories we tell and begin to tell here can help us to see ourselves more clearly as well as to see the gaps, silences, and spaces begging for stories still to be told.

Susan Goldberg and Chloë Brushwood Rose
July 2009

The D Word

BY MARY BOWERS

Sarah and I planned on a known donor from the get-go. My life has been a narcissistic pursuit of Self, and if my kid were going to do even half as much navel-gazing as me, she'd need to know both ends of her gene pool. Plus, we could pick the perfect specimen — a classical guitar-playing firefighter with rock-hard abs, if that wasn't asking too much.

But how does one acquire sperm, and once acquired, what does one do with it? Luckily, our local gay men's health clinic hosted a weekend alternative insemination workshop. We missed the first day of the insemination weekend where they must have covered lesbian conception. Sunday's topics were: international adoption, hiring a surrogate mother, and the financial considerations of having a child. The messages were, in a nutshell: good luck, good luck, and good luck. Financial Considerations Lady flipped foamcore graphs with huge red arrows pointing up, up, up. Her message: none of us could afford kids. Kids triple your expenses, she told us. Could any of us afford to live on a third of our current salary, she asked. That's a lot of cat food, and the lesbians huddled tighter. Financial Considerations claimed she and her partner wanted kids, but they could not yet afford to live on a third of their salary. I did not believe her. I didn't even believe she was a lesbian. The American Family Foundation probably planted her to scare the bejeezuz out of us gay breeder wannabes. It takes more than a mullet and black slacks to make a lesbian, imposter lady.

Because Sarah and I missed the first day of the insemination workshop, we didn't know how to make a baby. We didn't have sperm. We wouldn't have known what to do with the sperm if we had it. We needed instructions. This quandary brought us to our local lesbian-owned bookstore, where we found *The Ultimate Guide to Pregnancy for Lesbians*, the baby-making equivalent of *How to Tile Your Bathroom*.

"It *is* a turkey baster," Sarah said, reading Chapter 2.

It really was. Or a 20cc syringe. Or a 10cc syringe. Or an eyedropper. Or a soda straw. Anything seemed to do. The process was simple. Spread legs and insert sperm.

Now we knew what to do with the sperm, but we still didn't have any. We did have Jack Mott, and Jack Mott had sperm. Jack was not a firefighter, but he did teach high school math. Close enough. Jack was willing. Jack was able. Jack was cute.

We wanted Jack to understand the baby was ours. We wanted his sperm, and then we wanted him to go away. Except if we changed our minds and we wanted him around. Awkward! Coveting sperm is like going back to the best friend you told you would never speak to again, because you want to borrow her sweater.

But Jack was down with the plan. "I like the theory of bringing a child into the world," he said, "but the last thing I want is this kid showing up at my door looking for daddy to take him camping."

Yay, the plan was in place. I could be pregnant by the end of the month.

"I'm leaving for Paris next week," Jack said. "And I'll be back in six weeks. Then I'm all yours until November when I go to Prague for two months."

If I weren't ovulating in the seven-day window Jack was in the country, it would be four months before we could start. I was 36. I didn't have four months. It was hard to say good-bye to Jack, but we needed someone whose sperm would be ready at a moment's notice.

When Enrique offered to be our donor, I gasped. "You'll marry me — I mean, donate your sperm?" I said. Enrique was smart, funny, and dedicated his career to finding a cure for AIDS. It would be our good fortune to score his DNA.

"Absolutely," Enrique said. "I would be honoured." Enrique

wanted children; his partner did not. Donating was a compromise that satisfied Enrique's desire to procreate and Brian's desire not to have a child underfoot for 18 years.

"We got Enrique's sperm," I said to Sarah.

"He's not going to be out of the country for large chunks of time, is he?"

In fact, Enrique's sperm preferred to relax in their beautifully restored Victorian home where Enrique and Brian and their two Portuguese water dogs invited us to dinner to discuss sperm logistics. They served rosemary-grilled lamb, braised leeks, and morel risotto on their deck. Bottles of Pinot Noir were pulled freely from their wine rack. A jasmine bush puffed a cheery ambrosia across the dinner table.

"You don't mind signing away your parental rights?" asked Sarah, lamb speared on her fork.

"Of course not," said Enrique.

"And having no say whatsoever on how we raise the child?"

"I am bringing a child into the world," Enrique said. "There are a few things I would want to give input on."

Do tell.

"His name, for one. And the schools he attends. I would want to be present at his birth, or at least waiting at your apartment when you return from the hospital."

Wine glasses scraped across the teak table. Forks clinked against salad plates.

"Also," Enrique continued, "how do I know your relationship is solid? I don't want to bring a child into your lives and have you split up. I want my child raised by two parents."

"You don't want to be a donor," Sarah said. "You want to be a father."

He did. Our breakup with Brian and Enrique was awkward. Two strikes. Maybe it wasn't right, separating friends from their sperm. We turned to a community that valued sperm for its income potential: a sperm bank. For $400 we could purchase a glob of virility. No one waiting in our living room when we came home from the hospital.

"I want that one," I said, plunking my finger on the monitor. One donor alone, when asked why he donated his sperm, had written, "Honestly, for the money."

"He's direct. I like that," I said. Sarah was game; he had no acne. We bought Mr. Honesty's sperm. He got his money. We didn't get a baby. Four hundred dollars a month for fingernail-sized vials of sperm, more costly per ounce than white truffles, and four months later, we were not pregnant. Sixteen hundred dollars for something that was routinely sprayed on sheets, walls, and floors. It was criminal. I did not want teeny overpriced spermsicles. I wanted steaming buckets full of sperm, and I wanted them free.

We met Chip and Tom at our neighbourhood block party. They sat in matching canvas chairs wearing matching sandals, drinking Corona, and smiling. The Saturday before, Sarah and I had married on the lawn of our condo, and Chip and Tom knew all about it.

"We were out walking Bailey, and we heard *boom-shukka, boom-shukka* coming from your yard," Chip said.

"We said, 'That's got to be a gay wedding,'" said Tom.

"*I'm* telling the story, OK? So we said, 'That's got to be a gay wedding—'"

"And we stood outside your yard, in the rain, peering through your gate."

"Uninvited guests."

"We could see your tent, and people dancing."

"Was that Donna Summer you were playing?"

"We couldn't tell, we were so far away."

Chip and Tom were so disconsolate about not being invited to our wedding that we took them up to our condo, pulled out our wedding video, and pushed it into the VCR. Chip and Tom, our brand new best friends, sat through all three hours.

"Hey! This is where we came in," said Chip when he heard the warbled lyrics of "MacArthur Park."

"I wonder if you can see us in the background." Tom leaned toward the television and squinted. A man dancing with a gin and tonic balanced on his head appeared on the screen, and the picture went black.

"Now do you feel like you were at our wedding?" Sarah asked.

"We do feel better," Tom said, wiping his eye.

"Are you crying?" I asked. I looked over at Chip. He wiped his eye, too. "Are you *both* crying?"

"We cry," said Chip.

"It's what we do," said Tom. I have since seen Chip and Tom cry during *Sex and the City, Shrek,* and *Batman.*

Our friendship with Chip and Tom was forged over our mutual love of food and Sarah's and my singular love of people who watch our wedding videos. The first time Chip and Tom came to dinner, I served grilled steaks, guacamole, and tortilla salad. The following week they served salmon with mango chutney and cucumber mint soup.

"It's fresh mint," Chip said, watching us spoon our soup.

An exhausting volley followed: pine-nut-encrusted pork tenderloin, Irish soda bread, apricot-glazed lamb, hot and sour soup, olive-rubbed chicken, and three-chocolate mousse.

"We could order pizza," Sarah said one drizzly afternoon as I pored over cookbooks. I disagreed, and grilled shish kebabs in the rain.

Somewhere in the flurry of zesting, besting, and oohing and aahing, we told Chip and Tom our insemination story, including the sky-high sperm prices and acne-scarred donors.

"You can use my sperm," Chip said over spanakopita. "You can have as much as you want."

As much as you want. Chip and Tom were enthusiastic. Sure they'd sign a donor agreement. No problem signing away parental rights. Of course they would never tell us how to raise our kids. They lived across the street. They'd be available any time. They had no vacations planned.

"We want you and the child to have a relationship," we said. "We don't know exactly how that relationship would look."

"We'll play it by ear," Chip said.

"To playing it by ear," we agreed.

After a donor agreement and sperm tests, insemination began. Chip and Tom had moved — only a mile away, but on a block where parking was impossible. Sarah and I pulled the car up to the bus stop in front of their condo and waited while Tom helped Chip jizz into a bag. Frigid December air pushed against the car windows. I resented the air. Cold is the killer of sperm. We had twenty minutes to get the sperm home, up to our apartment, and into my uterus before they started dying. Tom flashed their living room light, and Sarah jumped out of the car and bolted up to their lobby where Tom met her with a plastic baggie of free, warm sperm.

Sarah and I were semen-challenged when we started. I thought we'd get a quarter cup of semen a pop. "That's it?" I said to the first sample Chip provided.

"That's a *lot*," Chip had said.

A few months in, I now knew that a tablespoon of the stuff was a *lot*. I revved the engine and eyed the glacially long red light at the corner. "Please be green when Sarah gets back," I said to it. The light was yellow when Sarah jumped in the car, and we tore around the corner under a deep orange glow.

"You got it?"

Sarah patted her coat.

"How does it look?" I said.

"I didn't look at it."

Chip's sperm was high quality. Our doctor had read Chip's motility results with a breathy enthusiasm, as if she wanted his sperm for herself. It's funny to revere the stuff I have avoided since the afternoon I gave Don Jackson a blow job in our high school stairwell, my last contact with semen. But here I was, reporting to Chip what we noticed about this month's semen: if it was particularly smelly, or thick, or abundant. If I had it to do over, I would simply say, "Thank you."

It took 13 months to get me pregnant. Thirteen months of one to three inseminations a month. We hadn't realized how enduring our donor relationship would be, or how much stamina it required. But the mechanical aspect of getting pregnant turned out to be the easiest part of our known donor arrangement.

Two months into my pregnancy, Sarah became convinced that Chip, the baby, and I would bond into some weird pseudo family, leaving her in the cold. Sarah got this idea from a story in a gay and lesbian parenting book. Two ecstatic moms and their adorable new baby attend the Christmas party of their known donor. The donor's friends coo and ooh over the baby, the birth mom, and the donor, ignoring the adoptive mom completely, leaving her to consume an entire platter of bourbon balls alone in the bathroom, her salty tears splatting against the octagonal tile floor.

The story blazed through Sarah's psyche, incinerating her confidence for the ten months of my pregnancy. Meanwhile, I was not receiving foot massages, breakfast in bed, or bouquets of roses. I kept thinking of Cher turning back time. If I could turn back time, I would burn that book before it came into our house. I was not worried about us being treated like a family. I was too busy worrying about realistic things like our baby being born with three heads, or with her heart beating outside her chest.

"I would really like you to read this book," Sarah said, shoving the offending thing at me.

"I've read the book."

"But you didn't read it through my eyes, to feel what I feel."

"Uh-huh." I wiggled my toes. They could use a massage.

"Furthermore, when I am pregnant, you will never know how I feel now," Sarah said. "You will have given birth, so you'll never know what this feels like." That irked Sarah, my never being where she was now. Sarah would never be where I was now — exhausted, with bloated feet, getting lectured on how un-pregnant she was.

My only concern was that once the baby was born, Chip would want to keep her. Chip could surrender his parental rights only after extensive interviews with the Department of Social Services. Even then, Chip had three days after the baby's birth to revoke his consent. If Chip revoked his consent, Sarah would have no parental rights, ever. "Sarah would remain a legal stranger," our lawyer told us. So Sarah and I were particularly interested in the outcome of Chip's three-hour interview at the Department of Social Services.

"How did the interview go?" we asked.

"So interesting," Chip said. "I loved Sandra. One of her sons is an ice skater; the other is in Little League, did you know that?

We talked forever, then she sent me to talk to her boss. Her boss and I spent most of our time talking about Rachmaninoff."

"The musician?"

"Musician, *ha*. Only the most famous Russian composer ever. We must have talked about Rachmaninoff — and my Cyrillic classes — for oh, twenty minutes."

"Did you talk about consent?"

"Oh, for sure. They must have asked a hundred times whether I was aware I was giving up my parental rights irrevocably. I don't know how many times I said 'Yes, I *know*.' Oh! And Sandra's husband is a somewhat well-known mathematician. Pretty interesting!"

As clear as Chip was that he had no intention of revoking his consent, Sarah and I mulled over the idea of putting Chip and Tom on a Caribbean cruise the week of my due date.

Weighing in at under five pounds, with lips like orchids and eyes like river stones, Jesslyn came into the world tiny, vulnerable, stunning. Chip did not revoke his consent. Sarah, Jessie, and I appeared with our lawyer in family court where a judge approved Sarah's adoption of Jesslyn. Everything according to plan.

Chip was a natural choice for Jessie's godfather and he stood at her baptism, resplendent in a purple shirt and lilac tie. Chip played the role of godparent-donor perfectly — present but not overly present. He hung back, perhaps to avoid the wail of five-alarm sirens blasting in my head. Sarah held Jesslyn at the font. Without Jessie in my arms, I felt unmoored, without a paddle, drifting. If Jesslyn were to identify Chip as her father, only one of us could be her mother, right? There was no precedent for a mommy and a mama and a daddy. In this three-minus-one equation, somebody had to lose. Who was going to get voted off the island? I didn't want it to be Sarah. More importantly, I didn't want it to be me. The priest rubbed olive oil on Jessie's forehead. Cameras flashed.

Poetically, we did attend the Christmas party of our donor and his partner, our four-month-old baby in tow. We stood in front of the spiky spiral wreath jutting out of Chip and Tom's front door and paused. What if the parenting book was right? What if the party turned *Lord of the Flies*?

"Hey guys!" Tom threw open the door, elf hat atop head.

Chip's friends did not treat Chip and me as the parents. In fact, Sarah and I were not in their picture at all. We gathered from the comments and restrained excitement that an entirely separate story existed between Chip and his friends: The Story of Jesslyn, starring … Chip!

"We heard that Chip watches Jesslyn while you guys nap," the friends said to us.

"He did that once," I said.

"And Chip *feeds* and *bathes* Jesslyn."

"On the two days a month he watches her, yes — he feeds her," Sarah said.

"And he's taught Jesslyn to sing. Amazing."

Behind us, Chip held Jesslyn, his friends piling up to him like a crowd of Betty and Veronicas pushing into Archie. Snippets of Chip's voice floated over to us: I feed, I bathe, Sarah and Mary sleep.

"I need to get away from this," Sarah said.

"Let's go check out the bourbon balls."

Sarah and I stood at the appetizer table, watching the crowd circle Jesslyn and The Parent of the Century. Christmas lights flicked on, off, on, off.

"Chip has given us a lot," I said. "We can give him this."

"I just don't need to listen to it," Sarah said.

"Hey," Tom walked up. "You girls haven't tried the flan? Chip made it."

We moved into a house, and our new next door neighbour, Rachel, hurled herself into my lap, announcing for the fifth time she was four *and three quarters*.

"That's nice," I said, extracting Rachel's head from my stomach.

Five feet away, Chip swung Jesslyn in wide circles, her tiny feet flying toward the sky as she squealed, "More! More! More!"

"Why does Jesslyn have two mommies?" Rachel asked, wrapping her arms around my neck. I don't much care for neighbour children draping themselves on me.

"Families are different," I said. "Our family has two mommies." We'd had this conversation before. Still, Rachel was silent, folding my answer over in her head like a paper fortune teller.

"But why?" said Rachel.

"There is no why."

Rachel stood up and walked over to Chip, fists planted on her hips.

"Are you Jesslyn's daddy?" she asked.

Chip's already wide eyes got wider. "Ah. " Chip gathered Jesslyn in his arms and turned to me. "Mary?"

"No, he's not," Sarah said, materializing out of thin air, garden trowel in hand. Rachel looked at Sarah, unconvinced but sufficiently intimidated to back away. Rachel turned back to Chip.

"Spin *me*," she said, extending her arms.

"You're too heavy," Chip said.

Rachel sat next to me on the porch steps, temporarily defeated. But if we thought we'd ended the baby daddy question, we were seriously deluded.

Jesslyn pointed to the man smoking a pipe on the toilet in *Everybody Poops* and said: "Mama!" She was two. Jesslyn pointed to the lonely bachelor who shoos bunnies from his garden in *Muncha! Muncha! Muncha!* and said: "Mama!" Dora the Explorer's mustachioed *papi*: "That's Mama!" Jim on *Lady and the Tramp*: "Mama!"

Soon I wasn't even *mama*; Jesslyn was calling me *daddy* and Sarah *mommy*. My heart broke. Did Jessie already feel incomplete without a father? Was I really that butch? Yes, I was, and I came to enjoy it. With two moms around the house, it's hard to differentiate your unique selling proposition. But as Jesslyn's daddy, I had a role. We wrestled. We kicked balls. We raked leaves. Daddy stuff. Only problem: I wasn't Jesslyn's daddy.

But neither was Chip. He sang to Jesslyn, made her brisket, and bought her first American Girl doll, okay. He blew raspberries on Jesslyn's belly and made her laugh so hard she'd fall over — daddy-ish, sure. But *daddy*? Chip spent five hours a week with Jesslyn, not exactly a daddy-worthy chunk of time, in our estimation. Chip was more than a sperm donor but less than a daddy. How to explain this distinction to Jesslyn? She was two.

"What do you tell your kids when they ask about their dad?" we asked our friends Tammy and Linda, who had three kids through a sperm bank donor. Tammy and Linda looked at us curiously.

"They don't have a dad," they said. "They have two moms."

"Do your kids ask about their dad?" we asked a lesbian couple at Gay Family Week in Michigan.

"Not really," they said.

"I love you, Daddy," Jessie said to me one afternoon. I took a breath. Today seemed like the day to tell her Chip was — ergh — her daddy. I was about to be voted off the island.

"Jessie, I'm not your daddy."

"OK, Daddy." Jessie said.

"Jessie, you have a special daddy."

"You *are* special, Daddy." Jesslyn wrapped her arms around me and pushed her cheek into mine.

"Thank you, honey."

"You're welcome."

Or maybe tomorrow was the right day to tell Jesslyn Chip was her daddy.

But Jesslyn didn't bring up the daddy question again until preschool.

"I sat with my daddy at school today," she announced, dropping her Hello Kitty backpack in the middle of the living room.

Alarm exploded through my skull. I crouched in front of Jesslyn and held her hands.

"*Who* did you sit with?" I asked.

"My daddy. The Spanish teacher."

"Jessie, the Spanish teacher is not your daddy."

"Yes, he is."

This was getting ridiculous. I muttered a serenity prayer.

"Jessie, Chip is your daddy."

"*Chip*?"

"Yes, Chip. How do you feel about that?"

Jesslyn shrugged. "It's good."

It was more than good. It was revelatory. It was Christmas, birthday, and Fourth of July fireworks rolled into one. "I have a daddy. His name is Chip," she told the postman. Jesslyn told her classmates she had a daddy. She told kids in the park, teenagers canoodling in front of our house, neighbours raking their leaves, shoppers at Home Depot. She shouted the news of her daddy, ecstatic, relieved. The only person Jesslyn didn't tell was poor Rachel, whose family had moved the summer before.

Amazingly, life went on as it had. Jessie did not become more Chip-centric. I was not pushed off the island. Jesslyn continues to muddle through her family configuration, alternately informing us, "I have a mommy and a mama and a daddy and a Tom," and "You can have two moms or two dads, but you can't have two moms and a dad." Jesslyn announces this without judgment, and I'd worry about it if she weren't so happy.

"What's in my Pop-Tart, strawberry jam or just strawberries?" she asks me from the back seat of the car, en route to kindergarten.

"It's actually strawberry filling," I say, pulling an answer out of my ass.

"How do you know?" Jessie asks.

"Because it has strawberries in it that *fill* the Pop-Tart, so it's strawberry *filling*."

"Like how you fill my heart with love?"

"Exactly like how I fill your heart with love."

"Like how the sun fills my shoes with glinting?"

"Exactly."

"I don't want to go to kindergarten, Mama."

"I know, honey."

Mamas' Baby, Papa's Maybe?

"How old is your son?"

I look up from the floor of the pharmacy, where I am trying to prevent my nearly-two-year-old son, Rowan, from stripping the shelves of their contents. He has an ear infection, one in a seemingly endless series of ear infections this fall. We've just come from the doctor, and now we're waiting for the prescription.

I locate the asker, a burly, bearded young guy in a hunting jacket, and I'm about to answer him, when I realize that his question wasn't directed towards me. Rather, it's been lobbed over my head to Rob, who is waiting with us.

Rob is not prepared for this. He fumbles the question, and misses. It hits him hard in the chest and then shatters and begins to drip — warm, wet — down the front of his coat and puddle in his shoes. He looks like a deer caught in the crosshairs of a rifle sight. He begins to stammer an answer, but is obviously too panicked to come up with anything coherent.

"Twenty-two months," I tell the guy, who glances at me briefly and then beams at Rob in what I can only assume is a guy-to-guy — a *dad-to-dad* — bonding kind of way.

"My little guy is sixteen months," he tells Rob, who has regained enough composure to smile weakly and nod. "But he's big! About his size." Hunting Jacket gestures towards Rowan, who has moved on to the homoeopathic stress remedy section. More nodding and smiling. A bit of toddler small talk until we get our prescription and make our getaway.

Of course, I think to myself, *this guy thinks that Rob's the father. He thinks we're the parents.*

And then I remember: *Oh yeah, he is. We are.*

Sort of. It's complicated. But not really.

Moments like these come up all the time these days, and we don't seem to be getting any more graceful at handling them. By "we," I mean me, Rob, and my girlfriend — my spouse, in fact — Rachel. If I try to strip things down to the barest, most rudimentary, of facts, the story would go something like this: Rachel and I wanted kids. We needed sperm. Rob provided. I got pregnant, had a baby, and a couple years later we did it all over again. And now there are these two beautiful boys, Rowan and Isaac. And they have two mothers. And a ... Rob.

Beyond that, depending on your perspective, things either get a bit murky or are crystal clear.

It's not that we're embarrassed or ashamed about the situation. It's not even that we're scared of the responses we might get. Before we moved from the big city to the small Canadian town we now call home, I worried that the spectre of a two-mom (plus gay male friend figure) family might be too much for the locals to handle. But they've all been great — have barely batted an eye. It's just that it's taken us a while to come up with an easy way to describe the situation in those blink-of-an-eye, waiting-in-line-at-the-pharmacy encounters. And so we stammer and nod and smile, stumbling along to the steps of the parental dance of recognition, searching for a language that somehow describes three (albeit unequal) partners instead of the assumed two.

On the surface, things seem relatively simple. Rachel and I are the primary parents, the hands-on, day-to-day people who live with the children, make the decisions about their lives, and provide the bulk of the care and the discipline. We're the ones on call 24/7, the ones — as we all agreed at the outset of this process — with all the rights, all the responsibilities. When we fill out forms, our names go under the slots for "parents" (or, maddeningly, "Mother" and "Father," which we cross out and replace with "parent.")

Rob is a man who went from being a friend on the further reaches of our circles to dead centre. He flew across the country for successive rounds of insemination, then for a baby shower, then to visit that baby as a newborn, and then every few months until a job opportunity opened up and he arrived to stay for a year, during which time we conceived and I delivered a second child. During that year, he saw us — Rachel, Rowan, and me — several times a week. He'd come over after work and roughhouse with Rowan in the basement while Rachel and I made dinner. Or *he'd* make dinner, arriving with groceries and Häagen-Dazs and elaborate plans. He'd use every pot we owned, and then stay to help clean up while one of us put Rowan to bed. He babysat. He set up intricate toy train tracks on our living room table, and helped Rowan navigate the cars around them. He made lattes and Pillsbury cinnamon buns every Sunday morning, and Rachel and I ate them on his couch while he and Rowan made forts in the bedroom. The day Isaac was born, a Saturday, Rob — so anxious — took Rowan for the day (and even managed to get him to nap) while I laboured at home with Rachel to support me. And when the baby arrived (a chance home birth) we called Rob first to tell him the name: Isaac Robert.

Which is to say that somewhere along the way Rob became our family.

But did he become a father? A parent? Or was he one at the outset? And how do you explain it all to the guy in line at the pharmacy?

Something jaded in me notes that so many so-called "traditional" fathers play the same role as Rob: show up for a year, or a month, or a week, or for dinner; roughhouse with the kids for an hour or two before bed; take them to the playground for the afternoon. They come and go according to the various forces — jobs, love, demons, desires, obligations — that shape their lives. And therein, perhaps, lies the difference between the boys' mothers and their Rob: for Rob, Rowan and Isaac are cherished, but only one of the many forces that shape his life at a practical level. For me and Rachel, Rowan and Isaac are, at least for now, the central force.

And that's okay. We and Rob agreed to nothing more — in fact, much less — at the outset. He never wanted to be a parent, has carefully refrained from offering his opinions or advice on the decisions we make, has never tried to suggest that he is an equal partner in this endeavour. Every visit, every hour of babysitting or roughhousing, every meal we share, every drink that he and Rachel and I pour at the end of the day when the kids are finally in bed — each of these acts has come about as part of its own, organic process. And we've loved it. Well, most of it.

But what does it mean?

If I could put it all on a T-shirt, I would. Instead of, "I'm with stupid," and an arrow pointing at Rob, I could have, "He's the *donor*, not the father. Sort of." Rowan and Isaac have both outgrown the baby onesie that declared, "I [heart] MY MOMS," but maybe we could silkscreen up new messages for them, things like, "My father is my other mother," or "We'll discuss later what to call our father," or "Nobody knows I'm the child of dykes (and a gay male friend)."

Of course, none of those does the situation justice, either. And, frankly, how much information is too much information? I mean, all the guy at the pharmacy wanted to know was Rowan's age, not his provenance. More to the point, I sometimes wonder who died and left me in charge of policing other peoples' interpretations of my family, "correct" and otherwise. Why do I care?

Because I do care, apparently. Not all the time, and not in every moment, but every so often it creeps up on me or hits me full in the face, the weight of all this invisibility, the way people work so hard to see what they want to see. Me and Rachel: Sisters? Two friends out with the kids? The "real" mom and the inconsequential one? Me and Rob pushing the stroller: a married couple, out with our children? (This is not my beautiful wife!) I chafe at the assumption that I'm straight, but it's awfully hard to blame people for assuming I am as I navigate the bookstore or the farmers' market or the pharmacy with the father of my children in tow.

Of course, there are the folks who just get it — at least, most of it — without us having to say a word, who beam at baby Isaac snuggled in the sling against Rachel's chest and congratulate the two of us on our beautiful children, the waitress at the greasy spoon who knows our orders by heart and tells us she remembers when her kids were the same age as ours, the little old lady at the next table who practically abducts the baby and then says, "Well, I *like* that," when we explain that we are both "the mom."

And then there are those moments of such pure acceptance that they veer straight back into "biology is destiny" territory: when people — strangely, almost always relatives — somehow imagine that Rachel and I are the biological parents of both children, attributing Isaac's blue eyes or Rowan's straight hair to Rachel's influence, so strong that it has somehow crossed the placental barrier and worked its way into our children's genetic makeup. And who knows? Maybe it has. "Yes, but, that would be improbable," I sometimes say, gently. Other times I just nod and smile. Occasionally, I slip up myself — as does Rachel.

And even though Rachel and I are the parents, and even as I am happy every time we are collectively recognized as the parents, even as I expect us to be recognized as the parents, there's this part of me that sometimes wants to say, "But there's this guy..."

Rob.

It's an adage central to the language of queer rights: love (as in, not simply legality or biology) makes a family. In fact, Rob himself has two fathers: a biological one, whom he refers to as his "father," whom he saw for the last time in his teens and whose funeral he didn't attend, and his "Dad," the gentle man who married (and later divorced) his mother and whose last name he took — and who disappears from his life for a months at a time. Rob of all people knows that biology doesn't make for fatherhood — and that neither does nomenclature. Maybe it's because he knows how easy it is to fuck up, how tenuous (and how relentlessly all-encompassing) this fatherhood game is, that he has opted to take on a role in our lives, and in those of our sons. Maybe that's why he moved across the country to be with us for that year, and is still trying to find a viable way to make our hometown his hometown. And maybe that's why he hasn't opted for full-time parenthood.

I want to come up with a tidy ending here, a way to sum it all up — ideally by inserting some anecdote that encompasses the innocence and wisdom of children, their uncanny ability to say precisely the right thing at the right time and, in so doing, clarify and simplify and crystallize our roles. But that would be a cop-out. In time, Rowan and Isaac will figure out what Rob means to them. In the meantime, Rachel, Rob, and I approach the question again and again.

Is Rob a father? A dad? An uncle? A parent? A very good friend? Something in between all of these? Is it that we don't know, or that language fails us when it comes to the words to describe our relationship? ("Rowan and I are ... related," I once heard Rob say to friends of ours, by way of explanation.) It's like those weeks and months of dating someone new, when you're not quite sure what to call yourselves, or the relationship. Partners? Lovers? "The person I'm dating"? So you try on different names and configurations, stand in front of the mirror and whisper, "my girlfriend," (or, months or years later, "my ex") until something shifts or clicks and you have a term, a definition, for what you are, at least some of the time. (Or not. I've also known people who go for years, for better or for worse, without managing to define the terms of what it is they're doing together. And, for what it's worth, 13 years into the relationship and four years into *de juro* marriage, I still can't bring myself to call Rachel my "wife.")

Maybe, in fact, it's just the opposite: maybe we're the ones failing language. Maybe it's that we lack faith in the ability of words to stretch and bend and accommodate our realities. If Rob is a father, does that somehow negate Rachel's status as a mother? If Rob is a father, then are his parents (his father? his Dad, whom I didn't meet until Isaac's first birthday?) grandparents? If Rob is a father, can he still leave for months on end, disappear for weeks at a time without phoning, choose when he will and won't visit, opt out of diaper changes and discipline and night feedings (assuming we relegated such tasks to him, which we didn't and don't)? It seems odd that the three of us, all of whom make a living via the written word, have yet to come up with a snappy answer to the questions posed by the well-meaning strangers in the grocery stores and playgrounds and pharmacies and restaurants that encompass our daily lives. It seems even odder that we haven't come up with a snappy answer for ourselves.

Or is it? None of us — me, Rachel, Rob — entered into this arrangement, this relationship, expecting it to be simple, uncomplicated. None of us wanted easy explanations, tidy answers. And, now, in the day-to-day rhythms of our lives — especially, and perhaps sadly, now that Rob no longer lives in the same city — it doesn't seem to matter as much. Rachel and I are Mom and Mom ("This Mom" and "Other Mom," actually, according to Rowan, who, perhaps, is the most pragmatic of the lot of us when it comes to dealing with language. Isaac, whose vocabulary consists of "Mama," "cat," "doggie," "yup," and "ta-ta," places a close second). Rob is, simply, Rob: at once viscerally important and ephemeral, vital and, somehow, optional.

But an option we chose. And an option we continue — always, always — to choose.

Donor Man

By Capper Nichols

The nurse turned to me and held out a sheaf of *Playboy*s. I hesitated, surprised and unsure. No one had ever pressed me with porn at six on a dark winter morning.

"Go ahead," she said, without a trace of coquetry.

I took the magazines and put them under my arm, like a stack of school books.

"You can use that room," she said, pointing across the dim hall. "Bring it to me when you're done."

It? My sperm.

A few minutes before, when I arrived at the hospital, I'd said to the nurse, "I'm here to..." I paused, unsure what term to employ. But she provided the proper euphemism: "... collect?"

"Yes," I agreed, but did not repeat the odd word, which to me suggested a scientific expedition to shoot large animals.

The nurse wrote down my name, the name of the sperm recipient, and handed me a specimen jar. Then she had remembered the *Playboy*s.

A few months earlier, two friends, a lesbian couple, had asked me to be their sperm donor. The initial (and tentative) proposition was made over email — I suppose to allow me time and privacy to mull over the idea. "We're asking you to consider being a donor/donating your sperm — the language is so terribly odd, cold and informal. We're asking you to help us give life to a child. How's that for a more dramatic rendering?"

I felt two ways about the request: embarrassed and honoured. Embarrassed because the people with whom I have shared my sperm usually haven't asked for it specifically. But also gratified:

you want *mine*? Maybe some biological imperative makes such a request powerfully flattering. Or maybe it's just vanity. But on being asked to donate, I felt compelled to flex a few muscles.

The couple, Susan and Rocki, had considered other donation possibilities, including one of Rocki's brothers (Susan would have the child) or an anonymous donor. But eventually they decided to ask me. They knew other lesbian couples who had chosen anonymous donors, but they preferred to use someone they knew — and someone the child could know. In the email they explained their specific choice by referring to my (and here I quote, from modesty) "smarts," "looks," "kindness," and, further, a quality of "openness."

What also contributed to my selection, I believe, was the fact that I am already a father of two daughters. My prior reproductive success proved I could deliver, but more importantly it suggested I would not prove grabby with the new child — occupied with my own kids, I was less likely, in theory, to become wistful about another. Any woman or couple who turns to a known donor must consider the risk that the donor will, once the baby arrives or at some later date, decide that DNA *is* a singular contribution and that he thus deserves a parental role. In recent years the news has been peppered with stories of second thoughts, and the subsequent litigatory baby tugs-of-war. Susan and Rocki made it clear that they would be the child's only parents. What I would "be" was negotiable, but the possibilities could not include "parent." I accepted this condition, assuring them that I could be trusted.

The hospital room was disappointing. I don't know what I had expected, but something other than a plain, antiseptic exam room: the usual vinyl bed covered with a swath of noisy paper, a couple of office chairs, a small desk in the corner. Unforgiving fluorescent light. Not what I considered put-you-in-the-mood decor. In the back of my mind I'd been picturing a venue more akin to Fanta-Suites. Say, a harem motif, with lots of pillows strewn about, attar of roses in the hot air, reclining odalisques dressed in gauzy, loose garments. Or maybe a NASCAR theme, a bed shaped like a stock car; the titillating odour of hot motor oil and burnt rubber.

But no. Just a room that spoke of cold hands and an impersonal demeanour: "How long have you had the cough?" and "What can you tell me about your recent bowel movements?"

I looked around, unsure where I should sit. No specific piece of furniture seemed designed to promote collecting. Should I stand maybe? That felt too informal for such a momentous procedure — too much like finding an out-of-the-way corner for an off-hand wank. My goal was loftier. I cast about for the collecting throne. Failing to find it, I settled for one of the office chairs.

But first I looked at the *Playboys*. I hadn't seen a *Playboy* for many years. Little had changed, though — maybe the hairdos, but the Playmate of the Month still shared her turn-ons and turn-offs in the same loopy, girlish hand. The opening pictorial in one issue offered arty black and white photographs of Katarina Witt looking the opposite of kittenish: an Amazon who could and would kick your ass. In another magazine, "Hef's Twins" were featured, two blonde and perfectly banal young women.

The summery glow induced by the magazines was enhanced by a certain urgency, the result of a five-day stretch free of recreational collecting. According to the written instructions for donating, which I had received in the mail, one must abstain for three days prior to the act of donation (but not longer than five, for some reason). I didn't know the exact day I would be called into action, but Susan had been able to give me a ballpark figure, and I had begun preparation through inaction. A little early, which might be credited to a rookie's conscientiousness.

I should pause here and describe the other, and much more important, item handed me by the nurse: the specimen jar. The plastic cylindrical container was about two inches tall, its mouth only slightly bigger than the circle one can make with forefinger and thumb. In my embarrassment over the *Playboys* I had not at first recognized the limitations of the container. But after unscrewing the blue lid and peering inanely inside, I realized the engineering flaw: a bit small.

This detail is not to imply anything about my dimensions, but only to point out that the narrow opening of the specimen jar offered an unexpected challenge. And here's the reason: I was simply not used to aiming. At the key moment I generally have not concerned myself with a precise target, such as the throat of a jar. On the contrary, this is a moment for a unique sort of oblivion — which doesn't lend itself to drawing a careful bead.

When the collecting moment arrived I did indeed find the target, but at the expense, I felt, of my best effort. I experienced something like a hitch or hesitation, which left me worried that my donation might prove insufficient. But what was done was done. I screwed the lid on tight and went out in search of the nurse.

"Here's my sperm," I almost said when I set the jar on the counter beside her.

Later Susan called and assuaged my worries. The doctor had been impressed with my specimen. "Oh, you got a good one here," she told Susan and Rocki. "One hundred and forty million strong, and impressive motility."

"Well, that's good," I said, with careful humility, as if the success of the procedure was my only concern. But what I really thought was, "Fuck, yeah!"

The first time didn't take, to no one's surprise. According to professionals and laypeople alike, it usually requires a number of attempts, especially for someone Susan's age, 37, and especially since she had never been pregnant before. Still, each of the first two cycles produced hope, and then disappointment.

The third time Susan insisted she had a good feeling. I had been out of town for a month, and would be leaving again for another month in a few days. The window of opportunity was small, but Susan ovulated, and I made a visit to the hospital. A different nurse, a man this time, handed me the *Playboys* and said something complimentary about Katarina Witt. The specimen jar was no bigger than before, but I had by this time perfected my technique, and I left the room feeling I had done my full best. All the same, the next morning I went to Susan and Rocki's house, at their request, and collected once again (in the privacy of their bathroom). They did a home insemination, piling on the sperm in an effort to ensure success. And sure enough, a week later Susan was confirmed pregnant.

A question of social etiquette: should one's role as donor be kept secret? I didn't readily share the info, but Susan and Rocki, who from the start talked openly among our friends about my role, answered the issue of disclosure for me.

Still, I hesitated to broach the subject. When others brought it up, I would try to look serious, but then smile sheepishly. In the months before Susan got pregnant, the first question was always some version of "Are you going to party or go medical?" I would slump my shoulders to indicate disappointment, and then admit to the artificial alternative. I probably went through this little skit a few too many times, but people seemed to enjoy it.

After settling the sex issue, questioners inevitably turned to the matter of parentage. "So how do you feel about *that*?" I would be asked, in an apparent reference to the fact that my DNA would be "in" a child not "mine."

The generally accepted notion is that donorship is a Big Decision. But it never seemed to me a momentous or solemn matter. I do not consider my genetic material sacred, or even particularly important. But I discovered that most people are uneasy with donorhood. Fine to pass DNA on to one's own kids, but sharing it about with *other* people's children (or to put it another way, sharing "your" children with other people) — that was a little disturbing. Most folks assumed I shared their reservations but had overcome my qualms in the interest of helping my friends. While many doubted the wisdom of my decision, most considered me laudable. I had shown myself to be generous and selfless; women especially responded with dewy-eyed approbation.

Which was nice, of course, but undeserved. I never did much soul-searching or moral wrangling. Susan and Rocki asked for some help; I said sure, I am all for babies.

And after all, I had plenty of sperm.

While I did not consider donorship a threat to my own emotional well-being, I did worry about my daughters' feelings. Before I agreed to donate, I had spoken to them both.

The eldest, Naomi, was 21 at the time, and living on her own. She saw no reason not to proceed; on the contrary, she was excited by the prospect of a new baby in our circle. Neither she nor I consider the genetic connection crucial or telling, no doubt because it's a link we do not share. We first met when she was nearly six, when I started dating her mother, Jenifer; at seven, when Jenifer became pregnant with my younger daughter, Alix, Naomi began to call me "Daddy" — and so I have been ever since. Our experience tells us that care and proximity are the makings of a parent-child connection, much more than the vagaries of DNA.

Alix, however, was less sanguine about my serving as donor for Susan and Rocki. One might have expected Naomi to be the one who felt threatened, but such an expectation would fail to consider Alix's age (14 at the time) or temperament: she is a worrier.

"So you won't be, like, the baby's dad at all?" she asked.

"No, the baby will have two parents, Susan and Rocki. The part I will play is small, if essential. All I have to do is —"

"Dad, I don't want to hear about that." She raised a hand and glanced away, as if warding off a blow.

(Later she admitted that at first she hadn't realized just what collecting entailed.

"What *did* you think?" I asked. "That they would cut me open and ladle out the necessary amount of sperm?" She had started to smile, but at the word "sperm" her features hardened, and she said, in a tone of warning, "Dad, stop.")

"Okay," I said. "We can skip that part."

A pause, then she asked another question, the one that worried her most: "But what if when it comes you change your mind? What if you really do love it?"

I paused too, wanting to take my time and give a careful answer, one that didn't simply dismiss her concern. "Well, I can love the baby," I said, finally, "but only like I would love any child of my close friends. You know? It won't be *my* baby. I won't live with it, take care of it, all that. That's what makes one a dad. I mean, aren't I Naomi's father?"

Alix nodded. Here was familiar terrain. We had talked before about the difference — the lack of difference — it made that I was not Naomi's biological parent.

"And I'm Naomi's father because we lived together, I took care of her. It's that simple. Just because my sperm is involved —"

"*Dad*, I told you, *please*."

Alix's questions revealed her single worry: would she be replaced? An irrational concern, it seemed to me, but I resisted an impulse to laugh. Bemusement and ridicule were inappropriate; I offered instead patient reassurance.

"The baby will not be my child," I repeated. "I have two daughters, you and Naomi. There are no more offspring on the horizon. *But*," I added, "even if I were to have another kid, you could never be replaced, Alix. That's not how it would work."

"You don't know."

"I absolutely do."

She did not grant me verbal agreement, but I could see in her expression — a slight relaxation in her features — that I had said what she wanted to hear.

Here's a confession, or maybe revelation would be a better word: before donating, I had participated in four pregnancies. No reason to go into the details of each episode — each of which is its own story, though some quite brief — but I name the figure because it signals my reproductive credentials. Which I find matter to me. They matter mostly because I want to keep open the option of becoming a parent once again, someday, maybe. At my age, in my forties, the option seems less available than at any other time in the last twenty-some years — partly because I am currently single, but mostly because I have passed through the primary reproductive years.

Susan's pregnancy was important to me first because she and Rocki wanted a child. But besides the pleasure of altruism, my successful donation also satisfied a need to be reassured about my own potency. One might say that the success soothed a glimmering of middle-aged crisis. But that would be facile, if not entirely incorrect. Such a crisis is supposedly ridiculous, and there is nothing silly about a desire for reassurance that one can still participate in the making of a child.

Susan and Rocki, during the pregnancy, sometimes joked that my services could soon be in demand in the local lesbian community, as they were hardly the only couple in their circles who wanted a child. I would laugh dismissively, as was expected, but I thought to myself, *I'd do it again, with the right people.*

If I seem flippant in telling of my donor-man role, this does not mean I took it lightly. But the *act* of collecting inevitably seems comic — mostly because masturbation in our culture is a familiar target of ridicule. As for collecting, the sperm bank has become a locale for teen boy sex fantasies, as in the dopey movie *Road Trip*, in which a curvy nurse assists a young donor by putting her thumb up his ass. My own storytelling participation in such fun is self-deprecatory — but not just as a way to talk about masturbation (about which I am generally reticent). I also mean to deprecate my part in the work that it takes to make a child — a small part indeed.

The male donor, I think, gets too much credit and attention; too much is made of his "feelings." If I were a surrogate mother, pregnant for nine months with a child I would pass on to another, *then* go ahead and attend to my psychological state, praise my efforts. But what did I do, besides come into a plastic jar? Well, I had to get up really early ... I couldn't masturbate for five days ... then I *had* to masturbate ... umm, I guess that's it. To be fair to myself, I also did give care to the donor moment, making sure to imagine only a proper desire, and not some untoward scenario. But of course it's hard to say if such piety mattered. For me, things got serious only once Susan became pregnant, once my part was done. Then there seemed a stake an actual person-in-the-making, not just an idea or plan.

In the months that followed, Susan's pregnancy made me nervous. Three years earlier, my then-partner, Michelle, had become pregnant. We had been "trying" and were both excited by the promise of a child, our child. But at three months Michelle had miscarried. The emotional aftermath contributed to the demise of our relationship. Since then, pregnancy had seemed to me a dicey prospect. I found myself reluctant to talk about Susan's pregnancy during the dangerous early months, afraid that somehow my attention would jinx her.

Once she began to show, I relaxed, some. Early pregnancy is akin to rumour, but a hard, rounding belly is evidence.

Over the months of the second trimester, and into the third, Susan grew slowly larger, more impressive in her pregnant bulk. When I see any obviously pregnant woman, I itch to touch her belly, usually a social *faux pas*. The pregnant Susan provided a rare boon, as she didn't seem to mind if I put a hand on either side of her mid-section and spread my fingers over the firm promise of a child.

On a Monday afternoon, almost nine months after my final collecting effort, Jenifer, my daughters' mother, called. "Guess where I am?" she asked. When I couldn't, she told me: "The hospital." For a moment I thought something had happened to her, but the excitement in her voice suggested otherwise. "Susan's water broke this morning," she said.

Jenifer had come out as a lesbian ten years earlier, and we hadn't lived together since. But we have remained close, and we share many friends. She had introduced me to Susan and Rocki, and she had moved in with them the month Susan became pregnant. She remained their housemate for the next year and a half, including the first part of the baby's life. During this same period, Alix, our younger daughter, lived full-time with me. Jenifer and I found this living arrangement more surprising than did our youngest, but Alix did not consider the baby — neither the theoretical creature nor later the real version — a competitor for her mother's affections; her lingering worry focused on the chance that the new child would draw me away.

That evening, I drove to the hospital. At the nurse's desk I asked for Susan. The nurse made a phone call, turning her back to make sure I didn't get any unauthorized information. When she hung up, she turned back around and said, "She's delivered, and they're taking visitors." She eyed me suspiciously, trying to decide if I qualified. "Just follow this hall," she said, finally, "all the way down to three-forty-six."

When I came to the room, I could hear excited talking and laughing inside. I hesitated. Should I be visiting so soon after the birth? Did I want to see the baby? After a long pause, I knocked. A moment later, Jenifer opened the door a crack and peered out.

"Hi," I said, diffident, ready to flee at the slightest hint of disapproval.

"It's here," she said, smiling, her eyes full with a weepy joy. "It's a girl!" She turned to ask Susan if I could come in. "Yes, of course, of course," Susan said, even though she was barely a half hour past giving birth. I sidled through the door.

Susan sat up in a hospital bed, her expression that mix of rapture and fatigue specific to newly un-pregnant women. A few spots of blood showed on the white sheet that covered her (too indifferently for my comfort). A nurse was closing up a bucket of the messier linen from the birth. Rocki looked surprised, as if stunned by her sudden good fortune. Susan held the child on her chest, and Jenifer said, "Come see."

Susan smiled at me, and then I stepped close to kiss her on the cheek. I looked at the baby, but not too closely, shy about peering at Susan's largely exposed breasts. After a moment I retreated to the corner by the door.

One of the nurses took the baby and placed her on a table near me and began to administer the post-birth checkup. She moved the baby's arms and legs to gauge flexibility. She gave her a shot in the thigh, and the baby gave a complaining cry — a sound like the faint whine of a wobbly kitten. The tiny child regained her composure, such as it was. She rolled her head from side to side. Her mouth worked, she blinked. She held her hands up near her face, flexed her fingers. So strange, so alive, one of us but utterly different. The nurse picked her up, and her hand engulfed the baby's torso; she put the child on the scales: five pounds four ounces.

I stood still, trying to imprint my shoulder blades into the wall. The room was full of women — Susan and Rocki, two other couples, Jenifer, a couple of nurses. The women took turns touching the baby, bending down to peer into her small face and babble baby talk. I divided my efforts between taking up a small amount of space and staring at the baby. Rocki used a cellphone to call her mother in Brazil and began to speak in Portuguese, her excitement readily translatable. I watched the baby ... and suddenly I *felt* a connection. The moment was fleeting, a catch in my chest, a whiff of almost sorrow, yearning here and then gone. I saw her as me, me as her, felt just a hint of what I had felt at Alix's birth. But the moment passed.

The nurse brought the baby back to Susan, so she could breast-feed. They worked together, Rocki too, trying to get the child latched on correctly. "Come on now," they said, and squirted a bit of milk on the baby's lips by way of inspiration. Susan's breast was three times the size of the child's head.

They named the baby Luca Maria, and I brought Alix to the hospital to see her the next night. Alix sat in a rocking chair, and Rocki placed the baby in her arms. Alix began to cry, and she could not stop. She cried and cried.

Later on the drive home, away from the hospital and the baby and other people, I wanted to ask, "Why did you cry?" But I didn't, instead letting the dark highway carry us along in silence. I cast about for some way of working the word "sperm" into a conversation, to distract her, but decided teasing was not a good idea just then.

Finally Alix said, "I don't know why I cried," answering the question I had not asked. "It was stupid."

I murmured my disagreement.

"It's not like she's my sister or anything," she said. She sounded surprised by the idea, as if she had not expected the baby to matter to her.

"She's not ours," I said, "and she never was. She's not coming home with us."

Alix turned in her seat and looked at me. "I know," she said. "And I don't even want her." There was something more, though, and she paused, thinking how best to explain herself. But she could not. "I don't know," she said.

Whatever the reasons for her tears, they did not come again in the ensuing days and weeks. On the contrary, Alix quickly lost interest in the baby. In part I believe she followed my lead. I kept my distance from Susan and Rocki, as I would any friends with a new child, leaving them to that intense and consuming time, an infant's first month. I did so out of respect, but also from proclivity (I find infants rather uninspiring up until three or four months). I assumed a slight, tangential role in the baby's life, and Alix seemed happy to do the same. Relieved, I would say.

After Luca's birth, more than one friend asked me, "How are *you*?" as if I had recently passed through a dangerous ordeal. The solicitude confused me. How should I be? Sad? Covetous? Maybe a little, that first night, but such feelings quickly passed, and within a few days those emotions were only a story I told myself about the birth. I was even a little relieved. Luca was, like all newly minted babies, a child who needed constant care and attention. And I had no patience or desire for that job. I could be happy for Susan and Rocki, and happy for myself too, the father of children who had long since learned to walk and talk and use the bathroom all on their own.

One morning, four months after the birth, I met Naomi, my older daughter, and Luca at a cafe for breakfast. Most times I had seen the baby it was like this — a glancing visit, a sidelight to some outing with Naomi, or sometimes Jenifer, both of whom occasionally cared for the child.

I had not seen Luca for four weeks, and her head looked markedly larger than I remembered. She slept in her car seat at our table but woke just when the food came. I took her on my lap, holding her with one hand, eating with the other. Her noggin dipped almost into my plate of rice and beans each time I leaned over to fork up a bite. For a few minutes the novelty of this rhythm entertained her, but then she grew bored and began arching her back petulantly. I put down my fork and placed a hand under each ridiculously tiny baby arm and passed her to Naomi.

A few minutes earlier, before the food arrived, I had thought, *Does she feel like "mine"?*

Not long after Luca was born I had visited a friend in another city, and I told him about her. He was very excited for me.

"That's great," he said. "You're a father again."

"No, it's not like that," I said. "I'm the donor. I wouldn't use the word 'father.' "

"But you *are* the father," he insisted.

I shook my head, said, "No, I don't think about it like that."

But it wasn't really that simple, father or not-father. What became apparent to me in those first months, even though I did not see Luca much, was that after all she was *not* for me just like other children not my own. I looked at her with a greater curiosity, and wondered about the ways in which we might prove to be alike. In appearance Luca took most after Susan, but we did look similar around the eyes. Time might reveal other concordances, and secretly I hoped it would.

When I had first agreed to donate I assured Susan and Rocki — and myself — that I would not, once the baby was born, try to claim a parental role. "We are not looking for another parent," Susan had said, and I had answered just as clearly, "I am not looking for another child." But though I spoke with confidence, I did not know for sure how I would feel when the child arrived. Once Luca appeared I was glad to be able to say no great change of heart had visited me. But neither was I unmoved. Instead something new seemed to have happened, something hard to explain. Luca is a different sort of baby for me, neither my child nor not my child. I have no familiar category for her.

She intrigues me, but still I don't want her. Maybe, like Alix, I fear that I could grow attached. But that doesn't feel like a true reason for my reticence. If I stay away it's more because we simply have separate lives to live. The intense dailiness between parent and child is for her and Susan and Rocki. I am her donor, not her father.

What it will mean in the coming years to be the "donor," I don't know. It may not mean much at all. For Luca there will be no great mystery. No, "Who is my father?" No dramatic meeting awaits us two decades into the future: the young, searching woman shows up on the grey-haired man's doorstep, they gaze into each other's eyes, the girl tries out a tentative "Dad?" and then they fall weeping into each other's arms; soon they are attending baseball games together, wearing matching shirts.

No.

Familiarity will diffuse the potential for drama — and trauma too, hopefully. But I imagine we will still eye each other with some specific interest.

My role is unfamiliar, yes, but not melancholy. I am neither indifferent nor sad, only curious about this new person and her coming years — and about what it will come to mean to be the man known as the donor.

New Path

BY CARRIE ELIZABETH WILDMAN

The first time I gave up my virgin status, I got pregnant. I was a classic 18-year-old After School Special, trying hard to walk the straight and narrow — maybe a little too hard. That first pregnancy, as unexpected as it was, set my mind on a new path. Always the rebel, growing up I swore I'd never do the marriage thing, never have kids. Swore it'd just be me, running solo, calling my own shots, on a farm with some huskies, changing the world with my art.

New path.

Once you know there's a little person growing in you, life changes. And once you wake up with the devastating realization that they are growing no more, life can never be the same again.

Midway through college, struggling with my sexuality and grasping blindly for my place in the world, God threw me another curve ball: a cancer scare. The prospect of possibly never getting to be a mother sent me into a panicked frenzy: *Babybaby-babyNOW*.... I was persistent, afraid. Maybe I overreacted. Maybe I was misinformed. Either way, I began to hyper focus. Either way I wasn't willing to risk it. Suddenly nothing else mattered.

Despite the fact that I was doing my time with the community psycho, despite having recently been outed — much to my parents' shame — by my two younger sisters (who thought my kinkin' around with girls was *cool*), despite being utterly financially unestablished, at the ripe and very fertile age of 22, I began to plot my new life of lesbo mommyhood. Still no desire to get hitched. I was still good with doing me, living my art, buying a farm. As for the huskies, I would have easily traded my violent, insecure girlfriend for a few good dogs. Live your dreams, right? Even so, young and naive, I went to her first with my brilliant desire. Madness mistaken for love.

Every time reality crept in, my unstable lover knocked it clear and far. "I have no money," I said. "Maybe I should just wait until I have a better job." *Maybe this, maybe that* ....

"You'll keep waiting, and it will never be the right time," she always countered. "Just do it." I think it was the most sensible thing she ever said. I took that one sign of intelligent life and ran with it.

We started keeping track of my cycles, buying up all the latest pregnancy books, referring to each other as "wifey," playing house proper — fights and all. I spent afternoons studying those hetero manuals, crossing out every reference to *husband, he, him*; irritated. That was me, taking a stand. Go figure. Daydreams swirled around those days of living someplace else, somewhere lesbian moms were embraced, not an oxymoron.

Psycho Chick girlfriend called from work one afternoon, dragging me out of my personal utopia. Her cousin was throwing a party and we were going — to look for baby daddies, no less. It never crossed my mind back then that it was anything but the most natural thing to do. It never crossed my mind that our prospects would have — let alone need — any say in our lesbionage-style plotting.

Later that night at the jam, we sat quietly at a table, watching the boys, critiquing them, whispering excitedly in each other's ears about their pros and cons, knowing nothing about any of them beyond what we could see and what snippets we could hear. Well into my second drink I was ready to flip into straight-girl mode and get my flirt on. Get my baby! By any means necessary! A clumsy, tipsy lesbian activist! What can I say? I was a cheap drunk back then. Still am now.

It didn't matter, though. There would be no need to fly into straight-girl mode. Most of the guys didn't give me a second glance. My "wifey"? All of her cousin's friends knew about her. Sitting with her I was out of bounds — a pretty new face, but gay by association. I was useless to them, a sad waste of fresh meat. And the ones that didn't know any better fell prey to some hot

Bajan cussing and quickly caught on. Poor them. She was an expert cockblocker and loved to exhibit her skills. I was untouchable. End of that. Shaking off my desire to crawl under the table, I refocused on our mission.

We added and crossed off dudes to our list throughout the night. Finally, we got it down to two contenders, then quickly to one. The Jamaican lightee had started acting all full of himself and calling out this pretty chick in front of everyone. Definitely not baby daddy material. Oh well, he was too short anyways. Psycho and I looked at each other and burst out laughing. "Next!"

Mixed Dude: my mom's fair complexion. Model type, nice smile, nice hair, funny-coloured eyes that looked light even in the dark. He was tall, lanky. Freckles. He looked harmless. "Babes ... we'd make pretty babies! I want him," I whined, slurring sleepily. Waxing off her fourth vodka cooler, she thought I meant her. She got this lovey-dovey look in her eyes, smiling for a split second — until she heard that last word: "him." Her face fell. Kissing her teeth, she dryly told me that her cousin knew the mixed dude. She'd get her cousin to ask. We were leaving. Just like that. My bad. Not a word on the drive home. She was sullen. Well, heck — that was better than vex. At least I'd get some sleep.

She left in the morning without waking me up in her usual (and sometimes twisted) way. So much for tradition. I shrugged it off. So, she was going to deny me my morning pleasures. Whoop dee fuckin' doo. A quick snapshot of the coming weeks of lonely, clit-throbbing, sex-free mornings came to mind. She was known to hold grudges. I was well seasoned. I'd live. Besides, it was Satur-day. Who in their right mind wanted to be dragged out of peace-ful-enough slumber at such an ungodly hour for hot sex anyway?

Oh no! What had I done?

Later that afternoon, as I was still enjoying having the house to myself, free of her sulking, her cousin called. He wanted to know why he hadn't been in the running. I don't remember what excuse I gave him, but some part of me, even then, knew I did not want Psycho Lover in my life all my life. Having her cousin's baby? Hell no, that was way too close for comfort.

Cousin told me he talked to his boy. He was excited, as though he knew he'd done well. "I told him, 'I know this chick who hasn't been with a guy in years,' " he said. " 'She saw you at the party last night. She wants to have sex with you — and she doesn't mind if she gets pregnant!' "

Doesn't mind?! Jeezus! *Why was he selling me like that? Doesn't mind?? What about the GAY part???* I was steaming, but I had to keep my cool. "Noooo," I said, trying to sound appreciative, yet stern, "... tell him you know a *lesbian* who wants to have a baby."

He didn't oblige. He told me he'd get his boy to call me, and *I* could tell him. *Fanfrikkintastic.* Panic began to set it. Thankfully, calm rescued me quickly enough. I mean, who does this? *He won't call. I'll have time to think this all through and* — the phone rang. *OHMYGAWD!OHMYGAWD!OHMYGAWD! Answer it before it stops ringing!*

I didn't want to answer it. *I did.* I didn't want to speak. *I did.* It was Mixed Dude! Words flowed from my lips as though some entity had taken control. I heard myself — cool, calm, nonchalant — talking to him as though it was the most natural thing, a breeze. I was out of my mind. Obviously.

Unfazed, my alter ego laid it all out, confident as she stressed the fact that I was a full-fledged, happily settled lesbian (*What??!*). Her voice hummed smooth and sexy as she cooed that my partner (*"Partner?" Bleh! cough! cough!*) and I wanted to raise a child together. She left out the Jealous Psycho bit, sold her as sugar-sweet instead. Smart move. I felt dizzy. Sometimes when I get nervous, I forget to breathe. Usually it's at the sight of eye candy. I think all the blood from my head goes to my... No, this was different. This was much bigger. Much dizzier.

After all was said and sold, he was still on the line. I could hear him breathing. No sarcastic remarks, no laughter. He was with it. (*He was— what??!*) I remember wondering what kinda crack this guy was smoking. *What's this guy's deal?* I waited for the "Ummmn ... yeah, hell no!", the "Lemme think about it," the *click.* Instead, he asked, "So when do you want to do this?" He was free later that night. I was freaking the fuck out.

Cool words flowed, even so. I'd have to call him back. I had to "consult with my [newly non-psychotic] partner" (*bleh! hack! hack!*).

Once the phone was safely in its cradle, I started to unravel. Logic was trying to bulldoze in, but I was in the zone! Okay, maybe I was in a daze, but either way, logic couldn't touch me. Not now. It was all so close.

My ears were numb. My mind was deaf. My head was spinning. I wanted to bang my head on the table. I wanted to jump up and down. I should have had a little sit-down chat with God. Instead, I called *her.*

"BABE! Thatguyfromthepartycalled!!! He'sfreeTONIGHT! Hesayshe'llDOIT!!! WHATAMIGONNADOOOWWWAH???!"

"Whaddayah mean, *what aryah gonna dewh?!* GO dewh it!!"

"WHATDOYOUMEANGODOIT!? WHYDON'T *YOU* GODOIT!? HOW AM I SUPPOSTA —"

"Gawdang! Yuh ovulatin', aren't yuh?"

What could I say? I was. *BAAAADDD.* Fourteenth day. I was *prime. That's the main reason I'm indoors! It's not SAFE to be in public! Someone could pass by me on the sidewalk too close, the wind could blow too hard, my pants might tickle my ... you know — or someone could look at me the wrong way and ... Well, no, of course nothing like that has ever happened before but—*

"Jump in...." My mind kept repeating the words. *I could do this.* I just had to psyche myself up. *I wanted this, right? I wanted this!*

Mind buzzing, I procrastinated, staring around the outdated kitchen. Suddenly, the peeling wallpaper fascinated me. The only sounds I could muster were sighs. *Big* sighs. *Suck it up, suck. On with it.*

I called him back. I'd given him enough time to get a clue. I called confident he wouldn't answer the phone. I'd be off the hook. He answered. I was hooked. I decided it must be fate. *Stop second-guessing, and just go with it.*

He came, picked me up. "Stranger danger" alarms? *Silent. Good.* I sat there in the passenger seat of his old Hyundai, inspecting him: *Freckles! And the eyes, were they green or — ? Wait! Holy smokes! Lookit those eyelashes! Okay, STOP! He'll notice! You don't want to give him the wrong idea!*

Speaking of wrong ideas, we decided to rent some pornos. I think we hit Blockbuster first. Yeah, wrong idea. He knew of another place. *Of course.* I suggested we hit the liquor store. He told me he brought weed. Sounding proud of himself, he informed me alcohol was probably not a good start for a baby. (*Heh?!*) Either way, it had been eons since I'd been with a guy. I needed some kind of inspiration. Green was good. I added my own less-than-wise wisdom: "Yeah, Bob Marley had hella kids. One spliff won't hurt." *Nice one, dingus...*

We were quite a pair. With our mutual show of brilliance, I wondered what our kid would be like. I stared out the window, reminding myself, *No second-guessing.* We headed up to my old place, east of the city. I hadn't been there much since I'd shacked up with Ms. Thang. As we got closer, I felt a weight lifted, a sense of freedom, anticipation bubbling up in me. *Or maybe it's gas.* I chuckled to myself, remembering that in all my nervous excitement, I'd skipped lunch. The weed was going to hit me hard.

Deep breath. *Think about something else, perv.* I stared back out the window, smirking. Something else. *Okay, well, he talks about his mom a lot, seems really polite and easygoing .... Wait, no! Do serial killers talk about their moms a lot?! Shit! What have I gotten myself into??!* I began racking my brain, trying to recall every cop show I'd ever seen. *Girl, stop! You asked — now receive, damnit!*

Home sweeter home. I was happy to be on my turf. Inside we planted ourselves in front of the TV, on the rattans. I glanced toward the bedroom, feeling a tinge of nervousness. *Damn, girl, chill.* Deep sigh. *You can do this.* Okay. Porno on? Check. Weed lit? Check. Musta been some of that Einstein weed, though. Instantly, we were pro porno critics, sucking back the green, picking the flick apart, talking about better camera angles, shaving pubes, to snip or not to snip, implants, life, first times. I was not feeling it at all. How was this going to work?

Then it hit me — that familiar tingling I'd been waiting for. First my eyes went higrade, then the body buzz burning down my spine ... *then* the sweet, sweet tingling downtown! *Ooooooh!* I could not hold back the goofy grin that came with it. Good to go! *Whew! Thank! You! God!*

"I'm going in the shower. Washrags — do you use those? I'll leave one out for you. Towels in there. Bedroom's there. Meet me in there if you still want to do this." My mind was in overdrive, words flying out before I'd had a chance to hear them in my head first for a once-over.

Deep breath. I got up, pressed play on the five-disc — Sade, on repeat. *"No Ordinary Love" indeed.* Smirking again. My friends will never believe this!

In the shower, I psyched myself up, lip-synching to Sade, slipping up every now 'n again and really singing, convincing myself he couldn't possibly hear me from the living room, only steps away. Dancing around like a fool, I did some last-minute vertical crunches. *As if.* Damn Einstein weed.

The bedroom was dark. It was always so nice and cool in there. Cozy under the summer duvet, I listened for the front door, part of me still thinking he'd leave. Moments later, I heard the shower, then after what felt like forever, the sound of him stumbling into my old room, commenting on the darkness, chuckling softly, trying to find me.

The rest of the night comes to mind in pieces. For the record, I don't listen to Sade anymore without cracking a smile. As awkward as its beginnings were, our baby-making was funny, lighthearted, comfortable enough — a weed-amped game of Doctor of sorts. He was a perfect gentleman, more than what I'd expected. All in all, I survived, the only downfall being the moments when I forgot in the comfort of the darkness and began searching for breastesez and cha-cha ... imagine my disappointment. I've always wondered if he noticed.

Soon after the deed, I remember feeling the sensation, like a pinch in my belly, like a little firecracker popping. No need for more. I knew right then, a beautiful future was brewing. I thanked Mixed Dude and rolled over sleepily; Psycho Wifey a distant nightmare, a smile creeping over my entire body.

I don't even know if I got any sleep. It felt like seconds later I was up with a start, awakened out of my blissful afterglow. He was still there. I recall thinking it strange that I felt so comforted by that, but there was no time to analyze it to the ends of the earth. The phone was ringing. Psycho, no doubt. Back to reality.

I answered reluctantly — from the living room. Yep, Psycho. No, *Hello honey, how'd it go?* either. She was pissed. Was he still there? Why!? "Oh, you want to be alone with him. Why'd you bring him there then, huh? Now you can have your happy little family!" The girl was tripping!

Her tirade grew more intense, words meshing together, devoid of anything civil. I sat there sleepy-eyed, speechless, perplexed ... very fucking confused. Wait a minute! Was I supposed to do him in her bed? Or wait! Was she supposed to supervise? What the hell? She wanted me to kick him out.

"I can't just throw him out!" I whispered angrily, suddenly wide awake. Just then, he stumbled into the living room, rubbing his eyes. "Are you going to sleep out here?" I shot him my best-attempt evil eye. *Grrrrrreat* — She had heard him. Another Bajan tirade I could barely understand ensued. Suddenly, I was straight again. Suddenly I didn't love her, and I was leaving her for him.

"Is that your girlfriend?" he asked, chuckling. "Do you want me to leave?" If not for his laughter, I would have mistaken the look on his face for concern. Even so, I was not kicking him out. The man had just given me my baby! I was sure of it! Besides, I did not want to deal with Psycho. Not now.

Wanting so much to throttle his sarcastic, pretty yellow ass, I cooled my rising temper, whispered to him that he could have my room. I was staying put. I waved him away, all the while muffling the phone. She heard. She hung up. *Damn ... here we go.* I expected to hear her banging down the door any minute. The way she drove turned city boroughs into blocks. She didn't show up.

She didn't call back.

I was tired, confused, relieved. I felt torn, but with Mixed Dude in the other room, as strange as it was, I felt safe. I decided to deal with the rest of our new life in the afternoon, sometime later, when my eyes weren't stinging, and I had washed his scent away.

Thirteen years later, I can't remember if he stayed the night or left. I do remember the look on his face when I told him I was eight weeks pregnant, though. It was July. We were at a funeral, of all places. I was there with Psycho Chick — sucker for punishment, I guess, young love at its most daft. *He* was there with his *girlfriend*. Yes. His *sexy as all hellll* girlfriend. Surprise, surprise... my baby daddy gentleman, not such a gentleman after all. Sexy didn't have a clue. I thanked God for my being a born-again lesbian and not having to deal with that shite anymore. *I* didn't have a clue.

All the while Sexy As Hell was around, Mixed Dude avoided me as though I had some terminal case of the cooties. When he finally did slip away to satisfy his curiosity, the look on his face was (pardon the cliché) priceless.

"Did it work?"

"I'm eight weeks."

If he could have jumped out of his skin, rewound the clock, or simply disappeared, I think he would have. He looked pale, shaken with disbelief, unsure ... scared? Note to self: *He never thought this was going to work*. With that realization, I felt an undeniable urge to smirk. *Men* ....

Life got stressful and complicated after that, far more stressful and complicated than the everyday average of living with Ms. Heckle'n'Hide. Mixed Dude had gotten a clue. He wouldn't sign the contract we had drawn up. He said he didn't want to risk his *parental rights*. It had sunk in. He was going to be a father. As for Psycho, she was in a perpetual state of jealousy over everything and nothing; an insecure mess of emotions; suspicious, vicious, volatile. All of this after *she* had insisted the baby would need to know his or her father. I just couldn't win.

As if all that wasn't enough to deal with, at 19 weeks I almost lost my little one. That was also around the time Psycho started bringing women home and staying out nights. So be it. Love had left long before, anyway. I shut her out completely. I was in survival mode. Life quickly became only about me and that little one struggling inside.

Beyond all of that mess, faith prevailed. I did win. Prayers make miracles, you know …. On a brisk February morning in 1996 I gave birth to a healthy, eight-pound, eight-ounce Chiney-looking, gorgeous little thing — a Heinz 57, just like me. So many years later, he's already taller than me, and I'm no shorty! He's a handsome, lanky boy, spitting image of his mama, not-so-mini version of his bio dad — mannerisms, thick black eyelashes, freckles, and all! He's got my chocolate brown eyes and is blessed with a huge extended family that adores him. All things considered, it's been a bonus to have the peace of mind of something more tangible than just a donor bio and photos on a disc to puzzle and wonder over years later.

People often ask if I would do it all over, drama and all. I would, especially knowing what I know now. I've had some simple regrets, but nothing that hasn't been voiced already to those that were affected. I wouldn't trade my beautiful, kind-spirited, witty boy for anything.

Me? Well, after three botched engagements (*I ran!*) and handfuls of mischief with various shades of eye candy, I've taken a hiatus from my widely acknowledged addiction to serial monogamy. I've taken time for me, grown up, realized in true Aquarius style the comfort of my own skin (after exploring every other possible alternative, of course!). Finally, it's just me and my boy, my art, my responsible 9ish-to-5ish (heavy on the *ish*) — a few dogs, and a farm to boot!

Psycho Chick is safely long out of the picture — or, rather, we are safely away from her and all the instability that filled those days.

Life isn't perfect, but it holds a certain dependable air of predictability in all the right places, and that's grand.

Now for the next mission! *Operation MILF.* Bio clock's a-ticking, honey, and my boy wants a sibling! He insists it's not too late.

I often tease him, asking what I'll do with some whiny little brat while he's away at high school and college. My darling boy, never stirred by my sarcasm, insists he'll "come home and watch 'em sometimes." He knows I'd love another li'l goofy face running circles around this farm just as much as he would. So cute!

Although his father is comfortable with the notion that having ample servings of cousins on both side of the family will suffice, I'm not convinced. The "only" children I knew growing up tell me today, as adults, that it's just not the same. That explains why they were constantly at our house, up in the mix, back in the days. Coming from a manic tribe that included one brother and two sisters, I can attest that there was not much sweeter back then than having a sibling around. We four were always readily armed for teasing, taunting, pranks, and battle scars. It was always great to have a rival nearby to blame for the latest mischief, too. And sure, even when I wished I never had them, I never really meant it.

Round two, I think I'd prefer a gay bio-dad, though, to save myself the ordeal of "jumping in." Someone handsome and stylish, intelligent, playful, dependable. Someone who would better understand where I'm coming from. Someone who will never try to kiss me when they see my girlfriend coming because their cousin dared them to (actually, looking back now, that was pretty damn funny!). Someone who'll never ask me to marry them and then not understand why I can't. Someone who will understand why I love them and take it for the pure and beautiful blessing it is, without getting it twisted. Someone who will roll their eyes, look the other way, and forgive me for the carnal look in my eyes when I'm ovulating — when they, like the rest of the hottie world, become fair game! *I wonder if there's meds I can take for that...?*

But, ah, yes! A gay daddy! We'd make beautiful Gucci babies! Okay ... maybe just *one*.

Donor Mom

By Tobi Hill-Meyer

When I tell people that I'm going to be a sperm donor, I always get the most incredulous reactions. You see, those who don't know me have no clue how a woman could donate sperm, and those who do know me know that I'm a trans woman who's had an orchiectomy — the removal of the testes. Either way, what I'm suggesting appears to be impossible.

What none of these people know is that I decided to make several "deposits" at a local sperm bank before starting hormones. Not many trans women feel inclined to do this, because it's expensive, and for some it doesn't jive with their sense of gender. But I had thoughts of becoming a sperm donor as far back as I can remember.

Since I was old enough to talk, I had been told about my own conception involving a donor and a turkey baster. I grew up knowing my donor and frequently hearing stories about my birth. Somewhere along the line, I decided that one of my life goals would be to become a second-generation sperm donor.

As a kid, one constant in my life was the fact that so many other people were interested in it. When I was born, the *San Jose Mercury News* did a photo essay on me. Lesbians had, of course, been conceiving with donor insemination for a while, but it was just starting to become big news, and everyone wanted to know what families like mine were like.

Once I hit age eight or nine, the questions started coming almost non-stop. In addition to the mainstream news, I was also a fascinating subject for academics, activists, and diversity trainers. The most frequent question was the one I found most confusing: "So, how is it having lesbian parents?" Despite having no other experience to compare my family to, I was still expected to come up with an answer.

I spent a lot of time thinking about it and gave what answers I could, most of the time explaining how it wasn't that different. Eventually, I realized that the unique and most significant aspect of my experience growing up with lesbian parents was that people expected me to be able to provide answers to an abstract question that few people my age would even comprehend. I gained a strong sense of introspection and a drive for analysis. However, I also became acutely aware of just how contentious my family was and how much of our well-being relied on other people's acceptance.

When I look back on things now, I can see even more that being subjected to other people's judgments had a strong impact on me. It most certainly had an impact on my parents. More than once they were hesitant to let me do something that they thought was perfectly fine but feared might look bad. When I was a pre-teen they sat me down to explain that I couldn't have sleepovers with girls anymore. We discussed how it was very heterosexist, but to do otherwise would look bad. I knew it was unfair, but it was a part of how we survived in a homophobic world. Similarly, my parents had been hesitant to let me wear pink when I was six. And when I came out as trans, part of their reaction (and mine, to be honest) was to fear that it might be seen by social conservatives as a reason not to let same-sex couples raise children.

Most of the questions I got growing up, however, were not from social conservatives, or even from well-meaning straight people. The group I got the most questions from was lesbians planning to have kids. They wanted to know all kinds of things. Did I get bullied at school? Was I out about having lesbian parents? Did I have supportive friends? Was the school system supportive? Their most pressing concern: "Is it better to have a known or unknown donor?"

I always did my best to explain that everyone's experience is different and that different needs created different preferences. My brother and I were perfect examples of that. For some reason, I — the gender-questioning, feminist, intellectual — was only ever picked on for being too much of a nerd. Meanwhile, my brother

— the straight, normal-looking daredevil — was constantly harassed for having dyke parents and was called a "fag" daily for two years. My only guess at explaining that discrepancy would be that we kept very different company.

In the midst of that bullying, my brother went through a phase of desperately wanting the status of having a dad. Luckily, he did have one. Unfortunately, his donor/dad had moved to another continent and wasn't all that available. But our parents tried hard to bridge the geography gap because having a male role model — and specifically a dad — was very important for him. I think it was a way for him to feel like he had some of the normalcy that his bullies harassed him for lacking.

The experience I had with my donor/dad, on the other hand, was more indifferent. I referred to him alternately as a "donor" or a "dad," and they both meant the same thing to me. From my perspective, it made sense to call him a dad while being clear that he wasn't a parent. I had no need for another parent of any gender, and I also had no need to deny the connection he and I shared.

One of the things I really appreciated about my dad was the story of how he became my donor. He had just gotten back from a gathering of male feminists and was terribly disappointed. He had seen many instances of racism, homophobia, and even sexism. Being so upset, he decided to write an article about his experience and submit the piece to a feminist magazine where my mom was an editor.

Thinking about the potential contacts he might have, my mom mentioned she was looking for a donor and asked him if he knew anyone he could ask. Now, my mom always told me that he immediately responded, "I'll do it!" However, according to him, he spent a few moments in silence, trying to think of anyone he could recommend. Since he couldn't come up with anyone he could trust not to become problematic in one way or another, he decided it was a part of his feminist duty to step up and help lesbians conceive.

That's about the best example of male behaviour I could have asked for. We moved to separate states, though, and as long as I didn't voice a need to see him, we only saw each other every few years. Given how infrequently I saw him, the issue of male role models came up every now and then in our household, as it so often does for lesbian parents. Once, before I was even aware that I was trans, my parents asked me if I might be interested in participating in the Big Brother/Big Sister program. Without realizing exactly what they meant, I began contemplating the possibility of being a big-sister type mentor to a middle-schooler. Once my parents clarified that they were suggesting *a big brother for me*, I immediately rejected the idea. I was happy to have the men in my life that I did, but I was certain that I did not want to have someone show up to be a male role model for me.

It was really useful to have my donor around when I began processing my racial identity. Being a person of colour raised by white parents, it was very useful simply to know my dad and be aware of some ways race had played out in his life. Given the limited opportunities we had to see each other, though, I now see how I could have benefited from some people of colour role models in my life. It seems ironic that my parents put so much thought into male role models I never wanted, while race was a topic we almost never discussed.

Having spent years trying to answer questions about the logistical ins and outs of lesbian parenting and donor insemination, I began to feel like an expert. Sometime in my teenage years I decided that I wanted to be a second-generation sperm donor. Jokingly, I thought if people were already coming to me for advice and perspective, why not become a one-stop-shop? In the end, though, I was simply proud of the way I was brought into this world. It made sense, in a cosmic way, to recreate the circumstances that had led to my birth. And being a sperm donor was my way of fitting into that.

This plan started making more and more sense as I got older and fell in love with my partner, Alethia, who doesn't ever want to have kids. As I planned for the lifetime that I knew we'd be spending together, I saw being a donor for a lesbian couple who wanted to have me be a part of their child's life as an excellent way to have kids in my life without having kids of my own.

When I decided I wanted to physically transition and take hormones, fertility was definitely on my mind. While it's not a reliable form of birth control, being on hormones greatly reduces fertility. I knew that it was possible to go off hormones for a few months and be capable of producing functional reproductive material, but going off and on hormones is not a fun thing to do. My doctor wanted me to wait eight months after making my decision before starting to take hormones, so it seemed a good time to freeze my sperm.

I didn't want to get into all the details of my gender with the fertility clinic, so when I called I just said, "I'm about to undergo a procedure that might make me infertile, and I want to freeze sperm beforehand." When I went in, I aimed to pass as male. Given the context, that wasn't too hard.

During my consultation, the nurse explained the details of the process — and the expenses. Afterward, she sent me off to the bathroom where I could, um, produce a sample.

"And in here," she unlocked a small cabinet revealing a stack of pornographic magazines, "are some materials in case you need any help."

I glanced at the covers and was stunned by how straight everyone looked. Their makeup and lingerie somehow made them appear even more straight than the straight women I interacted with on a daily basis.

Medical offices have always been stressful places for me, and the pressure to perform in a small room with a sink, toilet, and laminated floor certainly didn't make it easy. Not surprisingly, the provided "materials" were of absolutely no help. I realized that it might be unreasonable to expect them to have queer women's porn. It *is* harder to find, and how were they supposed to know that they were freezing a dyke's sperm? I did note the complete lack of men in the magazines. Were they in complete denial about the chances of having a gay man as a donor, or were they just too afraid of scaring the straight guys?

Thankfully, Alethia was able to come with me the second time. After that, they started giving me a sterile cup so that I could do it at home. I had to do it in the morning before either of us went to school. Then rush it to the clinic. Despite the time crunch, it was a lot more relaxed. It also felt a lot better to be engaged in procreative work while in the arms of someone I loved. Call me sentimental, but I'd much rather have that kind of energy involved than the nervous tension of a clinic bathroom.

By the end of the process, it had become a lot more expensive than I had prepared for. While mild compared to other procedures that trans people often undergo, the nearly thousand-dollar price tag obliterated my savings and left me with just enough for my living expenses. Having waited so long for my chance to start hormones, I worried that I might not be able to afford them. Luckily, that didn't turn out to be the case. While testosterone blockers can be expensive, estrogen itself is fairly cheap.

From that point on, I wasn't in any rush. I wasn't specifically looking for anyone to be a donor for, but now and then a friend would mention looking for a donor, and I'd mention myself as an option. Most times, it was a hypothetical, years-down-the-road situation. Even then, half the time it became clear pretty quickly that we weren't the right match for each other. In one case, a friend who had a lot of men in her life was a little perplexed as to why I would offer frozen goods when she could get someone to deliver it fresh.

But that was okay. My own standards had gone up since my potential as a donor had gone from hypothetically infinite to 23 vials. While I might have been okay being a donor for someone who wanted no involvement on my part before, I now found myself more concerned about the choice. Would I approve of their parenting methods? Would we live within easy travelling distance? Would we share similar values? Would we be family? I didn't have a checklist of qualifications, but I found myself questioning in a lot more detail what I would be okay with.

A couple of different friends made tentative plans with me. They didn't want kids now, but perhaps in a few years, and wanted me to keep them in mind for such a possibility. Simple plans like that became a little more complicated when one of those friends became my lover. Ronan and I dated for a few months, and then, about the time that Alethia and I had a handfasting ceremony, we invited Ronan to come live with us.

One day Ronan asked me if I wanted kids of my own. My plan had always been to be the donor/frequent babysitter. I'd never before had a partner who was even hypothetically interested in raising children. But being a sperm donor for a lover who lived in the same house — while not being a parent — didn't seem quite realistic for me. That's when I began considering the possibility of being a primary parent. And while the time and financial commitment seemed a bit overwhelming, there were definitely aspects of the idea that seemed very appealing.

For one thing, Ronan is also queerspawn. The idea of raising a kid with four queer grandparents seemed fun. And since we are both trans, something about that just seemed magically right.

Over the next few years, as the idea percolated, more and more of my friends started having kids. I found myself cooing over every baby and cute little kid I encountered, in what Alethia called "baby lust." And suddenly, all of the tentative planning finally formed into reality. We're still biding our time, at this point. The way things look now, our life circumstances should be right in the next couple of years.

I stopped looking for anyone else to be a donor for, and we just continued living our lives. That's when I met Deana and Sasha. I had placed an ad on craigslist for, of all things, queer or queer-friendly gamers to teach me to play Dungeons and Dragons. They were a couple that I had previously met at a local LGBTQ meeting. Before I knew it, Alethia, Ronan, and I had formed a gaming group with the two of them, and we set out on an almost-weekly adventure that lasted a year.

We talked about all kinds of things, started going on hikes and kayaking together, and all became close friends. So when Deana and Sasha mentioned that they were looking to get pregnant — and having difficulty finding a donor — of course I brought up myself as a possibility.

It turned out that I actually fit their criteria more than most of the people they had already asked. They hadn't thought of the possibility of asking me, well, because it's not often that you think of women — even trans women — as potential sources of sperm.

As we talked more about the possibility, it became clear that not only was I a good fit for them, but they were also a very good fit for me. They liked the idea of having their donor stick around, and given how close we were as friends, they asked Ronan and me to be godparents. They would have asked Alethia as well, except for the not-wanting-kids thing.

I had also been concerned about the role my parents would play. A person I had previously had tentative reproductive plans with had been very clear that he didn't want to share any child he birthed. "I don't even know if I want *my* parents involved," he had said, "let alone yours."

Given the problems he had with his family, his position had been perfectly reasonable and I supported it, even if it wasn't what my parents had hoped for. In contrast, though, when I cautiously mentioned to Sasha and Deana that my parents really like kids, their quick and enthusiastic response was, "We'd love to have an extra set of grandparents."

So now I find myself about to continue this family tradition. And just like my parents before me, the family we're about to create is going to be even more complex than the models I grew up with. We'll have two moms, a godparent, a donor/godmother, the godmother's partner, and six to eleven grandparents — several lesbians, bisexuals, trans people, and genderqueers among us — and a half-sibling a few years down the road. Yet as complicated as that can seem when placed in a list, it's really very simple: we're a family.

Unexpecting

BY ROB GRAY

When Rowan was born, I was on a writing retreat in a cabin on the west coast with another writer. The moms had told me when they thought the C-section would be, and I paced the dock, where I could get the best cellphone reception; paced the cabin; couldn't sleep. When more than a day had passed, I could barely breathe. Sitting in the rain at the end of that dock, I feared the worst. And the worst wasn't just that the baby might not be well, but that I had, unbeknownst to me and to the moms, contracted and passed on HIV or some other disease to him and to Susan.

As a 39-year-old gay man, I have for all of my adult life been inundated with messages about discrete bodies, about safety, about containment. So when Rachel and Susan asked me to help them make a family, to be unsafe in so many unexpected in ways, it was a blind "yes," like agreeing to go to China based on the principle that you like the food and have heard great travel stories.

Susan and the baby, Rowan, were both fine. The moms couldn't reach me because I was in the wilderness, and, truly, they were otherwise absorbed. In the light of that, my fears concerning Rowan's birth might seem irrational. Granted, I am a little more neurotic than your average pansy. And I didn't know that Susan had gone through a barrage of tests, including an HIV test, in her first trimester. But there is always risk.

I am a safer sex-guy. I've only ever had unprotected sex within the confines of monogamous relationships. Still, there is risk: "safer" does not mean abstinent. And, not wanting to base my entire sexual life on fear, I manage that risk. So there was still a chance, in my mind, that perhaps I did not manage that risk well enough, and that I had put Susan and the baby — and maybe even Rachel — at risk.

This is what we do. We manage risk. I've watched Rachel and Susan, and through their example I have learned. When do you let the child climb — and maybe fall — and when do you tell him not to jump on the furniture? When do you let the child run on ahead, and when do you make her hold your hand? You take responsibility for the risk. Because if you want to believe in safety, in security, you have to acknowledge the unexpected.

Two and a half years later, on the brink of Isaac being born, the man I last loved calls. He tells me he's just found out he has HIV. I am immediately two people: the one who wants to fly across the country and hold him, hold him down, let him know this isn't the end of anything for him, that he will still be loved, by me and others to come; and the other me, paralyzed with panic, trying to do the math, gently asking when he thinks he seroconverted, trying to remember when we conceived, racking my brain for anything, for moments I might not remember, moments that might have been riskier than I imagined.

I was paralyzed with fear. My worst fear. Not that I had contracted the virus, but again that I might have passed it on to Susan and the baby.

I wondered if I should get tested first, and then tell Susan and Rachel when I had more information. I'd been trying to help, trying to be there more in those waiting moments, in these last weeks of the pregnancy. I didn't want to bring this to them, to add worry and stress when, despite my fears, it might not have been necessary.

I decided that it wasn't my choice to make. This was one of those things, those risky things, from which I could never entirely protect them. I took it one step at a time, moving across the hallway at our mutual workplace to tell Rachel. We went home, their home, and I told Susan.

The living room became a tight holding, no air. The kind of tense thickness before a thunderstorm, when it seems impossible to break. Sodden with weight.

Many of us are like this. We watch movies knowing that, unlike the protagonists on the screen, when the comet comes, when the train races towards us, when the bear attacks, we will sit down and watch our fate come towards us. All those disaster-preparedness videos be damned. And so, in the living room across from them, I sat and cried.

In my memory of this moment in time, the two of them are knitting the air, the madness of what we are going through, sorting the twines into sense, regular and careful. Rachel later refers to this as the burden of care. I remember watching them shoulder it, first one, then the other, passing it back and forth between them in the thick air. Maddeningly, they keep asking how I am. I think they're insane.

We do the math. We measure when it was my ex must have contracted the virus, we measure when we got pregnant. We account for what we know: that during the attempts I did no more than kiss and even after we got pregnant had "safer" sex, nothing too risky. We do the math. But there are still things we don't know. We call the midwives to consult test results. I am leaving for Vancouver in two days and will see my doctor there and get one of the instant tests. We do the math.

I am paralyzed. My fear and horror slip to awe and back again, and then to awe once more. Do you know this? Do you know how strong women can be? Their hands moving in the thick air, not pacing, but sorting. Folding. Smoothing it out. Like they had already imagined all these possible tragedies, and were prepared for what they could do. As I sat, shell-shocked, staring dumbfounded at their hands passing this back and forth, they worked through the steps of the worst-case scenario: how will the baby be, who they need to warn, how will Susan be, need to talk to the midwife, how will I be, how will my ex be? This is what they shoulder, what they pass back and forth, worrying the spots that need worrying, smoothing the tablecloth over the flat table.

In the gut of all this, I see what I sensed about them from the start. How they could do this thing, this thing I knew I couldn't quite do. I don't know for sure that this is true. Maybe I'd be the parent who could through sheer adrenaline lift a car off a child. But here we were, in the deep depths, and they were doing it, while I watched, crying, staggering from fear to wonder.

Isaac was fine. Susan was fine. I'm fine. And even the man I once loved and his current boyfriend — his husband, now — are fine.

Still, this is what we do. We shoulder the weight of care.

When Rachel and Susan were pregnant with Rowan, our first son, I was researching psychics for a writing project and attended a psychic fair in a hotel ballroom. By the end of my afternoon, I had seen two psychics. Both had predicted that in the next year I was going to have a child and both noted that it would be a boy. When I told them that I was gay, they said it made no difference. Of course, I liked best the psychic who told me I was going to get married in the next year. She seemed wise beyond her years, and that was saying something.

Four months later, the baby shower for Rowan and a family reunion coincided and I opted for the baby shower. In the wake of my mother's wrath, my brother and I shared a phone call. "You're starting a family now," he said. "You have to think of them before you think of anyone else. It's like you're married to them now." Married. There it was. Prophecy, as Macbeth and I both know, is a bastard.

I have spent a great deal of time along this journey with worry. Since I no longer live in the same city as Susan and Rachel and the boys, I have become acutely aware of arriving and departing, of what I bring and what I leave. And as much as I have moments of feeling *in* it, my perspective these days is more outside looking in. More intimate than the teenager who delivers the *New York Times* (two days late in their small town) but less than the four of them, there in the trenches. I worry about what I take with me, what I might take from the boys. I worry.

When people find out I am a donor dad, then find out the moms and kids are in another city, the first thing they ask is "How often do you see them?" It's a simple but loaded question. I answer and then I avoid looking at their faces, avoid seeing them calculate and deliberate and find a verdict: am I a parent or more like a Unicef sponsor, getting smiley photos in the mail? I remember the threat I heard from so many moms when I was a kid: "Just you wait until your father gets home."

Our fathers then were defined by their absence. Am I any different?

But I avoid their faces because I, too, in my own way, judge my absence. And worry.

In the wake of our scare, Susan commented on my sense of responsibility for everyone, the sense she got that I felt compelled to shoulder all the weight, the burden of care, the responsibility for all that was happening. I've done enough therapy to know where it comes from. I'm sort of textbook that way. But I remember it in them too, in the early days, the worry with Rowan and his inability to sleep through the night, the fear that they might make a mistake and harm him. But children, like mothers, are tougher than they are made out to be.

This last visit, I was in their backyard with Rowan — now nearly four — holding his arms, swinging him through the air, both of us laughing, breathless. On the periphery, I could see Rachel stop what she was doing on the deck, freeze. When I brought Rowan back to the grass so he'd breathe again, she quietly asked, with a nervous chuckle, if that could be the last round. I nodded. I knew Rowan was safe all along, my hands the ones holding him, but from where she stood there were the irrevocable facts of her child and the ground and the space between them.

When we say yes to questions we can't imagine the answers to, when we let these small conundrums of happiness climb blind to gravity, and when those little, way-too-cute sneakers run on ahead without us, I know it's not just their risk we manage. So I remember Rachel on the deck, her breath held up under her clavicle, waiting for the spinning to end, for her child's feet to be on the ground again, and know the risk is one thing, the sense of responsibility a whole other. And I remember sitting across from them in the living room, their hands moving in the air, not controlling the chaos, but nudging the unnecessary out of the room, out into the yard and alley, making room for more air.

And in that space, and the spaces since then, I've realized why, what I knew when they first asked me to be their donor, why I said yes without knowing what I was really saying yes to: Rowan and Isaac need no more than what they have. They are covered in love. They swim in it and drink it in by mouthfuls. They don't need me. The love I have with them will be just what we choose it to be. Just like Rachel and Susan don't need me. We all get to choose, choose this love. This is the unexpected: the way I have fallen in love with these two women. The way I've become part of a family. And Rowan, giggling in the grass, his mother finding her breath on the deck, says it better than all these words as he calls out across the yard to her and to me, staggering on the grass, dizzy from spinning: "Again!"

Father: Not Stated

BY AARON SACHS

The drawer squeaked loudly as I pulled it, startling me. I paused, my heart beating quickly. I listened, and after a few minutes, let out my breath: I hadn't woken my mom.

"Goddamn," I muttered to myself, annoyed at both the drawer's crotchetiness and my own jumpiness. Once again I reassured myself that what I was doing wasn't really wrong. Still, were my mom to come downstairs and find me rifling through her filing cabinet at midnight, I'd be hard pressed not to feel like a busted cat burglar. Carefully, I resumed pulling on the red metal drawer, more slowly this time. It opened to me reluctantly, as if it sensed the small fortress of guilt in the pit of my stomach. Even though the files I was looking for were *technically* mine, or at least *about* me, I still felt guilty

With the drawer fully open, I stopped to listen for movement in the bedroom above me. Again, nothing. I began thumbing through the tightly packed files. Most of them seemed to contain tax returns, some of them mine. I didn't, however, see any files boldly labeled "Aaron." I was about to give up when I noticed a hanging folder labeled "Children." Inside were several smaller manila folders. Most of them appeared to be the records of my brother's taxes and bank account, but one bore the faded mark of a blue felt-tipped pen: "Documents." I lifted it out, taking care to use the hanging folder to mark its place.

The folder contained several official looking documents: my brother's birth certificate — the original and several copies — and a handful of other documents. Only one of them pertained to me: an uncertified photocopy of my birth certificate.

At the sound of the upstairs bathroom door closing, a cool wave of panic passed over my body. I was concentrating so completely on the documents that I hadn't even heard the bedroom door open. Quickly, I closed the folder and held it over the drawer, ready to replace it if I heard footsteps on the stairs. I reassured myself once again that there was no need to panic. After all, I had a plausible reason for snooping.

"I got a call from a lawyer today," my mother told me. My brow furrowed, my arm mechanically pushing a spatula across the skillet as I sautéed mushrooms and onions for dinner. I pressed the phone tighter between shoulder and ear.

"Your father wants to meet you."

Pause.

I stopped sautéing the mushrooms, the word "father" hanging in the air with the scent of frying butter. I knew I needed to say something, a response to bring the moment to a close. But I couldn't think. The words lay motionless between my ears: heavy and slippery. A tingling began working its way up to my stomach and through my body, a sensation — something like the lurch of lost gravity on a roller coaster — the physical feeling that I've come to associate with an emotional one. Except this felt more like a baseball hitting me in the testicles, doubling me over in slightly delayed agony. Normally it takes me a few minutes of feeling myself out to determine exactly what that emotion is and what's at its root. I needed to speak, though.

"Oh," I said.

Pause.

"Uhmmm, alright," I added flatly, sensing I needed to say more. Very lame. I always imagined myself responding with amazing ease and eloquence in situations like this. I felt justified in my bungling, though: my mind didn't have any way to process the information or provide me with an even halfway appropriate response; there was no precedent or model, no previous experience for me to go by.

"You know you don't have to meet him if you don't want. It's up to you, Aaron." Under normal circumstances, I'd find a statement like this irritating. Of course it was up to me, I wanted to shout. It was *my* father we were talking about. The ball of chaos rolling into my stomach and the dull ache that accompanied it, however, overshadowed the brief flare-up of annoyance.

"Yeah ... I know," I replied. After a pause, I added, "Uhhmmm, I guess I'll need to think about this some."

"Of course. I'll call up and get some information ... "

"No! I don't want to know anything yet," I interrupted. "Nothing."

"No, that's not what I meant .... Why don't I just give you the number for the lawyer, just in case. I'll call him up, though, and let him know that you have his number." There was a slight pressure to her words, but I ignored it.

I stirred the mushroom and onion mix once or twice before putting down the spatula to retrieve a pen and scrap of paper. I could hear my mother talking, but I was stuck on her previous statement: My father. No, not my father, the donor. I couldn't call him my father without a lot of connotations that I didn't want. "The donor" sounded more neutral, more sterile. She was saying something about what she'd said to the lawyer, what he'd said to her, what she would say when she called him. I couldn't really hear her. My eyes and ears had tunneled, locking on the piece of paper that seemed to squirm under the pen I held awkwardly. She gave me the lawyer's name and number, each digit taking forever to scratch out, barely legible. I looked at the scrap of paper and then slid it out of sight on my desk. Not now.

"I'm just glad I could give you this opportunity, Aaron. I'm so appreciative of that." Fuck that, I thought. I wasn't glad. I hadn't asked for this. Ever since I was 18, I'd known that if I really wanted to, I could track down the donor. It was my decision to make, when I wanted. Now he was forcing the decision on me. I felt a distinct loss of control. I swallowed my anger. No, not now.

"Hurry the fuck up," I whispered, my arm getting tired despite the folder's minimal weight. My skin tingled as production got underway in my sweat glands. Finally, I heard the footsteps retreat to the bedroom, the door close, and the creak of the bed. I relaxed and immediately felt stupid for being nervous. There should be no reason for my edginess. Nervousness was a gateway drug to guilt, the two connected in a feedback loop. I tried to shrug it off and opened the folder again, pulling out my birth certificate.

Name: Aaron Dickinson Sachs.

Sex: Male.

This Birth (Single, Twin, etc.): Single.

No surprises there, thankfully. I think most kids secretly hope for a long-lost twin, and many that do have twins secretly wish they didn't. A good friend of mine was adopted close to birth. When he got older he found out that he had been a twin, but that his twin had been aborted. The mother hadn't known she was carrying twins and by the time she realized she was still pregnant it was too late. I often wonder how my friend can still be pro-choice with a story like that, but he is. Our birth stories sit opposite each other, the unplanned and the extraordinarily well-planned. I kept reading the birth certificate.

Place of Birth: Samuel Merritt Hospital, Oakland.

Time of birth: 8:28 in the morning. I'd always thought it was 8:25. There used to be a clock in the living room, frozen hands pointing out the time of my birth: 8:25. For a while I thought that, through some kind of miracle, the clock had just stopped on the day I was born. Later on I found out that it was just too much work to keep it wound and so they'd put the hands at eight and five. I guessed I'd have to change the clock.

Age of Mother: 36. My moms, now separated, met in the Bay Area. Nikki, my biological mother, had come to Berkeley in the early seventies from New York on a hippie school bus. She came to work as a therapist in one of the Free Clinics and probably because Berkeley was still a centre for leftist politics at the time. Jean, my other mother, moved up from Southern California first to finish school at Stanford and then to go to Berkeley for graduate school.

Name of Father: A decisive, "Not Stated." It would have been more accurate for them to put down "Unknown," but I figured it was probably a pretty standardized thing. It wasn't a surprise; I have never had a father. It's too bad they couldn't have put "Name of Additional Parent," but that might have been a little too progressive. Even in Berkeley, a lesbian couple having a baby in 1980 was pretty radical, especially a boy baby. I knew that there were at least one or two children born to lesbian couples in the Bay Area before I was. These were the pioneers; the handful of advanced scouts before the first wave. I was in that first wave.

In 1979, my parents joined up with a support group for lesbian couples that were thinking about having children. Not for women planning on having children: for women tentatively considering thinking about planning on having children. Out of this group, my parents were the only ones to make it on to that next step. Of course, there was another support group for women actually having babies, and my parents joined that one, too. What they did take away from the first group, however, was an increasingly strong friendship with another lesbian couple. Since my parents were the only ones who made it to that next step, this couple decided to help. I still didn't understand why this couple chose not to have a child themselves. Maybe they were waiting to see what would happen — like when you let a friend eat the food first to see if it tastes good before having any yourself. But even then, after my parents had a child, this couple chose not to have one. My mom once said it was because after I was born, my parents became too boring.

This couple was charged with finding a sperm donor for my parents. At the time it was difficult to work with sperm banks if you weren't a married, heterosexual couple. Up until the late sixties, artificial insemination was still legally defined as adultery, regardless of the consent of husband and wife. The Sperm Bank of California, which my parents used to have my brother, wasn't around until 1982, and they were the first to serve lesbians and single women. So these two women were our sperm bank. The donor was anonymous. My parents initially wanted several donors so they could mix all the sperm together — that way they wouldn't know who the actual donor was — but it turned out to be difficult enough finding just one eligible donor. Confidentiality agreements were made, although not formally. He had a physical and filled out a short medical history questionnaire. Working through the other lesbian couple, my parents acquired the donor's sperm, and they inseminated at home. After two inseminations, I was conceived.

While my mom was pregnant, my parents spent a little while on names. Not on what they'd call me, but what I'd call them. In a lesbian household, there's no taking titles for granted. If not planned right, it gets confusing quickly when a child yells "Mom." Since my parents had decided to raise me as a Jew, they thought the best thing to do would be to use the word *"Emah,"* which means mother in Hebrew, to indicate Jean, and "Mom" to indicate Nikki. I'm sure when they made this choice it was based on Nikki's being my bio-logical mother; "Mom" somehow seemed more natural like that. I sometimes wonder if maybe they should have switched the two. If they were truly dedicated to both being equally my mother, then Nikki's claim to "Mom" would be no greater than Jean's. Besides, Nikki was the Jewish one, not Jean. Of course I refer to both of them as "my mother" in conversation, something that's been con-fusing people since I progressed beyond baby burps and gurgles, but I do my best to distinguish the two when it's appropriate. I guess it's hard to get away from some traditions, even in an untraditional family. Nevertheless, armed with names, a lesbian support group, and probably two copies of every psychology books on parenting ever written, my mothers were ready for a child.

I was born on the morning of July 17, 1980, at around 8:25, no, 8:28. It was a long labour. My moms tell me that I was a furry baby. I had a crusty coating of hair on my head and more coming out of my ears. They say I looked like a little werewolf. I lost the hair almost immediately, thankfully. There's a photograph I have of me as a baby, sitting on a couch surrounded by other babies. "The First Generation of Lesbo-Kids," I imagine the caption would read. These are the babies of the lesbian support group. I'm one of the oldest in the picture. For the most part we look happy, sitting there dressed in an assortment of the muted autumn colours popular in the early eighties: lots of browns, lots of velour. There's something historic looking about the photo. And, in a way, it was a historic moment, if not for the gay and lesbian community then at least for my parents. Sometimes I imagine that the photo is proof of some kind of scientific research that was conducted. A Cold War experiment, we children would find ourselves blessed with extraordinary intelligence, super-human strength, or some host of special abilities that would manifest themselves at puberty. Too much TV. Too many comics. For a short while I tried to convince myself that the werewolf ears had been a sign at birth of things to come. That didn't happen either. Maybe it's better that way. There were already enough things that made me different without having to add werewolf to the mix.

I was tempted to take my birth certificate, but I didn't want my mom to notice its absence, at least not yet. Of course, I could legitimately tell her my curiosity was fueled by the news of the donor wanting to meet me. I slipped it back into the folder and the folder back into the cabinet. Better to avoid the subject altogether. Sometime soon I'd get it back out or make a copy. But right now my mind was occupied with something else: the donor. I hadn't looked at the "Medical History Questionnaire For Sperm Donors" since hearing the news. I knew there was a copy in my desk upstairs, so I gently closed the cabinet and, turning off the desk lamp, headed for the stairway.

Once in my bedroom, I turned on my light and sat on the bed, looking at the desk. The questionnaire now had more weight, and I was hesitant to shoulder it. In the past, I'd had more distance from the document. In college I would often joke about it with my friends or the girls I was dating. "Hey, would you like to meet my father?" I'd ask. When they gave a confused affirmative, I'd go into my room and produce a double-sided sheet that I'd hand to them. "X, I'd like you to meet my father. Father, please say hi to X." Maybe the joking was just a way for me to emotionally detach, to create a comfortable distance. Now, even saying the word "father" was too real. I repeatedly felt the need to chastise myself for not using "the donor" instead of "my father," out loud and in my head. Especially in my head.

"This is silly," I said to myself, "it's just a piece of paper." I got up and crossed the room, quickly, while the idea was still fresh. I opened the drawer. I could see the protective plastic sheet I kept it in peeking out from beneath some receipts, my old fake ID, and a box of unopened condoms that were more than likely long expired. I pulled out the questionnaire and, making sure not to look at it, crossed the room again to sit down on my bed.

"Alright, Aaron, you're halfway there," I continued to coach. "You've got it in your hands, now you just need to lift it up and look at it. How hard can that be?" I sat there for another minute before realizing that neither my neck nor my arm had moved. I wanted to yell at myself to look at the document, but I knew that would wake my mother, so instead I closed my eyes and tried to do some meditation exercises I'd learned from a friend. It didn't really relax me, but closing my eyes gave me the courage to lift the paper up. "You've looked at this paper so many times. It's not any different now, so stop tripping about it so much," I reassured myself. "It's still not going to tell you a lot." I thought back to the last time I'd looked at it, perhaps two years earlier. "He's nearsighted and has hay fever." For some reason those two facts had always stood out to me. I think I'd even included them in my college entrance essay.

I slowly opened my eyes and looked through the protective plastic sleeve at the document inside. It looked exactly the same as it had the last time I'd taken it out. Yet, it felt different. I felt like this piece of paper was all that stood between the donor and me: his presence growing more palpable, as if he were just on the other side of my bedroom door, waiting for me. I could pretend I wasn't in, hope that he'd leave, but I knew sooner or later I'd have to come out of my room. I'd have to face my father, or at least his absence, and what that meant to me.

I slid the page out of the sleeve, wanting to feel the paper in my hand. I'd read the questionnaire before but never tried to understand the document itself. I rubbed the paper between my thumb and forefinger, trying to glean something from it, but it felt like paper. I lifted it to my nose. There was the vague smell of a copy machine, the way paper smells when it first comes out and is still hot. Looking at it, I realized it wasn't even the original. More likely a copy of a copy. It was just a piece of paper: my father.

Of course, there was a story tied to the Questionnaire. Probably several, for that matter. There was the story of the donor, a story I didn't know since I didn't know him, and there was the story my parents told me. Soon after I was born, my parents decided they needed to update their wills. Not being legally married — they hadn't even had a commitment ceremony as was popular among gay couples in the mid and late 90s — there was nothing to guarantee that Jean would be granted custody of me in the event of Nikki's death. They also realized that were something to happen to both of them, they needed to name guardians for me. They chose Nikki's sisters. When the lesbian couple that had helped my parents acquire sperm found this out, they were extremely angry with my parents.

"Why didn't you name us as Aaron's guardians in the event of your deaths?" they probably said. "Have we not been there since the beginning, supporting and helping you make this decision into a reality? Did we not provide the sperm for his conception?" I don't know if they used these words, but the idea behind them is clear: "We should be his guardians since we've done so much to make this happen." I can imagine the women, angry, sitting across from my parents at the dining room table.

"Listen," my parents would reply. "He's our son, and we want him to be raised by members of our family. While we consider you really good friends, you aren't family. We want Aaron to be raised Jewish. We want him to have his grandparents in his life. These aren't things that would work with you as the guardians. We appreciate all of your help, it's just not clear why you should feel so entitled to be his guardians." No reply.

I've often wondered this too. Why did these women feel so entitled to me? Why did they see it as a friendship-ending decision? My parents have hypothesized that it was because the donor was related to one of the women; that they *were* in fact family. One of the women had a brother that for a long time was the prime sperm suspect. I've always been dark-skinned, darker than the other members of my family. (I'm also the tallest man in the family, not including my Norwegian second-cousin once removed who still has me beat by two or three inches, but whom I exclude on the technicality that he married into the family.) This brother would have been Greek, something that my parents felt would explain my dark colouring. For several years in elementary school and junior high, I became obsessed with Greek mythology. I never claimed to be Greek; I never even consciously associated my interest in mythology with the paternity theories of my parents. My interest was still obvious: I spent a week in the library trying to learn Greek.

While I may have unconsciously believed my parents' hypothesis as a child, their explanation never fully satisfied me in adulthood. If they were so invested in being involved in my life, as evidenced by their response, the lesbian couple could simply have revealed the donor as a relative. Doing so would inevitably have caused some problems, but it was within the realm of the possible. Rather than get stuck on the identity of the donor as the key, I've tried to understand the position of those women and their reaction. They were surprised and hurt. For them, it was only natural that I would go to them. These people were intimately involved in my conception. On a symbolic level, *they were* my father. They were the source of one half of my genetic code.

"Mom, I think I'm black," I said to my parents one day. Without any hard facts about the donor's ethnicity, my parents had little in the way of a counter-argument other than to point out that I did not — at all — look like I was black. I was dark, but olive-skinned, I've-been-baking-myself-in-the-sun-for-a-good-couple-of-days kind of dark, not biracial dark. Still, I wanted to believe it was possible. In an effort to answer some of my questions, my parents decided to contact the couple and ask for more information. They wanted to know the donor's ethnicity and perhaps more detail about his background. They wrote a letter explaining what they wanted and why, for my sake, it was important.

Not long after that, my parents received a letter in the mail from a lawyer, who informed them that they would be in breach of a verbal confidentiality agreement. Were they to continue pressing the issue with his clients, they would get a restraining order against my parents. So Jean and Nikki never again asked the couple, hoping instead that one day I'd have the chance to find out more on my own. After all, *I* had never agreed to the confidentiality of the donor.

But that wasn't why I was looking at this piece of paper now. I was taking stock of what limited information I did have; to remind myself of what I knew and see if there was anything I'd previously missed. I was surprised at how much like a painting this document was, every person seeing something different. I remembered the first time a friend took a look at the questionnaire.

"Wow, so your dad was in his forties when he donated," he said.

"What!" I replied, and hurried over to where he was. "Where the hell does it say that?"

"Uh, right here, at the bottom." I looked at where he pointed. Right on the first page, under other disabilities or ailments, it listed the arthritis his mother had in her sixties, the Parkinson's his father had in his seventies, and the gallstones the donor himself had in his forties. Like a decoder ring, my friend's finger pointed to information that had always appeared to me before as simply medical, but was now clearly revealed as more personal.

"Damn, I never really noticed that. I mean, I've read this whole thing a number of times, I even had it on my wall in high school for a bit. Right under the Bill of Rights. Somehow I never realized his age was right there, staring me in the face." I stood there for a minute, letting the information soak in. "So wait," I said. "That means he was ten years older than my moms."

"Yeah, sort of. Forties could mean anywhere from forty to forty-nine though."

"True, but 'forties' implies that some of those years have

passed, right? Let's just say he was forty-five, for argument's sake, okay? Right in the middle of the range."

"Sure, we can say forty-five. Why does it matter, though?"

"Well, my mom was thirty-six when she had me, and that was kind of old for a woman to be having a child. For anyone to be having a child for that matter, at least at that point in time. I think it's also pretty safe to assume that anyone donating sperm for artificial insemination is probably not married. It's possible that he was, but I somehow doubt the guy's wife would be down for him to be impregnating other women, even artificially."

"Alright, I'll let you make that assumption," my friend said, looking only slightly skeptical.

"Well, if he's not married by the time he's forty-five, it seems pretty unlikely that he would get married and have kids after that."

"Hold on a second. First off, why couldn't he have been married *before* that? Second, I don't see why it's so hard to believe that he'd have kids in his late forties or even early fifties?"

"That first one's a good point. He could have been married before donating. Still, it seems unlikely to me that he'd donate if he already had kids. I guess what I'm saying is not that it's impossible, but that it's unlikely. I'm speaking in terms of probability."

"Okay, it does seem *unlikely* that someone who was already a father or married would donate sperm for artificial insemination."

"Right. And given that he was in his forties when he donated, it's probable that he never got married. Therefore, it's also probable that I'm the only child he's got."

The thought stayed with me for a little while, and a couple of weeks later I got the chance to talk about it with my mom. I was heckling her for not moving in with her girlfriend, and somehow we ended up talking about cohabitation and then marriage.

"Well, I pretty much grew up without marriage being a part of my life. It's not in my genetics. I mean, I don't think my fa... uhm... the donor was ever married," I said.

"Really?" she said. After a pause, "Yeah, I don't think he was married either."

"Wait, why don't *you* think he was married?" I asked, wanting to know if her reasons were the same as mine.

"Well, I've always thought that he was gay."

"Seriously?" I asked. "Why do you think that?"

"I think it came from that donor questionnaire. Isn't there something that talks about abstaining from sex?"

"Yeah, it's at the end. It asks if he'd be willing to be tested for VD. I still think it's funny they said 'VD' instead of 'STDs.' Definitely points to the age, I guess. Anyway, it says he'd be alright with taking a test before donating and then abstain from sex during the period of time he had to donate."

"Right, that's what I was talking about. The way he says he'd be willing to abstain from sex, he makes it sound like it would be difficult to do. It sounds like he has sex a lot." The words came out slower, more self-consciously, as she said the last sentence.

"Wait a minute, I think I see where you're going with this . . ."

"Well, it sounds a little stupid now that I'm saying it out loud."

" . . . You're saying that he sounds promiscuous, and of course everyone knows that gay men and promiscuity go hand in hand like bagels and cream cheese."

"I'm stereotyping, aren't I." It was more a statement than a question.

"Yeah," I said, elongating the word for emphasis. "And you're the lesbian. God, *Emah*, shouldn't you be more open-minded? I'm the heterosexual man here. If either of us is going to say something like that, it should be me."

"Hmmm," she said, breaking into a quick laugh. "Well, I guess you're right. I shouldn't be making those kinds of stereotypes. But hey, I'm a different generation."

"I just think you have this fantasy of him being gay because it really rounds out the family situation. I mean, that would kind of make sense: *boy raised by lesbians finds out he has gay dad.*" I used my best announcer voice, but my mom didn't seem to notice.

"Do you have any fantasies about him? About who he is, or what he'd look like?" she asked. At first I thought she was just trying to change the subject, but the tone of her voice and the expression on her face suggested she was serious.

"Well, not really. It may be surprising, but I've kind of tried to stay away from that most of my life. I figured it wouldn't really help me any." I knew my mom wanted to ask me more. I could see she was trying to open up a space where I would tell her more than I normally would, and that my answer wasn't really what she was looking for.

"Well, I've always had my fantasy. I imagine him as a tall but slim man with dark hair. Kind of like you. For some reason I've always pictured him in flannel, like a plaid shirt or something."

"Okay, so first you say he's gay and then you say he wears plaid flannel shirts? You really need to work on your stereotypes, *Emah*."

"Yeah, again I realized it didn't sound quite right when it was coming out of my mouth."

"I think you're just mixing stereotypes. Flannel plaid is what the dykey lesbians wear. It matches the mullets they all have."

My mom let out a big laugh.

"Okay, so maybe he doesn't wear flannel," she said. "What I was meaning to say was that I imagine he's rugged and outdoorsy."

Sitting on my bed, the questionnaire in hand, I tried to figure out if my father — no, "the donor" — looked rugged. But it was still just a piece of paper.

After Yes

BY ANNEMARIE SHROUDER

My home is spotless. I even cleaned the baseboards. You are coming over, and I want your first impression to be a good one. Not that I would raise the baby in this place, but my home is a reflection of who I am, a little more of me. I want you to like what you see and feel comfortable here.

This will be our second meeting. The first time we met, you agreed to be my sperm donor. We sat in the park until it got dark, eating ice cream, my dog lying close by. The conversation was effortless. We discussed what I wanted (a known donor with no parental rights and responsibilities, but who would be part of our lives) and whether my vision fit yours (it did!). We talked for a couple of hours — about families, ourselves, and the journey we were embarking on together. My cheeks hurt from smiling. I was composed on the outside, dancing on the inside. "This feels safe," you said when we parted ways, and I agreed. I was elated, but not surprised; I had had a feeling about you.

That was a month ago. Almost exactly. After that talk, I sat quietly alone at home for a long time. I tried to write, but no words were adequate for the gratitude and quiet I felt. You had said yes! Nights spent wondering were over: would I ever find this man? Am I asking too much to find a donor I like, trust, feel good with? Am I crazy to go this route? Would I know, and would I trust my gut when I saw time passing by and my age creeping up? Gone also were the months of seeing mothers with babies in the park or passing them on the sidewalk, and wondering if that was ever going to be me. I said thank you out loud and in my heart that night, over and over again.

I thought that I'd want to tell everyone, but I found that I wanted to hold the news close; to keep it just for me for a while; to see how it felt to be one step closer to conceiving and having a child, and to have found the man who would accompany me on this journey. It felt more peaceful than celebratory; an internal *"yessss."* When I finally went to bed, I couldn't sleep. I felt like I was going to burst with joy. One three-letter word from you transformed me into a mom-to-be, and brought this dream so much closer I could almost feel this child waiting to be born.

I read over my journal to discover with amazement and delight that I have found exactly the person I described 29 months earlier: a man I like, respect, and admire. A man of colour. I say a quiet thank you to the universe and tread softly in this new place where longing has no home, and I can begin to prepare to be pregnant.

I read the conception section of *The New Essential Guide to Lesbian Conception, Pregnancy and Birth*. I learn more about my body in those chapters than I have in 38 years of living and 17 years as a sexually active adult. They should teach us how amazing and perfectly we are designed to conceive — or not. Echoes of "be careful" and fear of pregnancy rattle around in my memory. If only I had known my body better then, I would not have been so afraid of desire. I would have felt it more, experienced myself more, been more spontaneous. I feel sad and cheated that my body and my sexuality have been more of a mystery than a source of pleasure, and make a mental note to teach my daughter about her body so that she can enjoy it.

I schedule a naturopathic appointment, and I photocopy a chart to track my fertility. I buy a fertility lens to check the changes in my saliva that show when I'm ovulating, and a speculum to monitor cervical changes. It feels strange to be so consciously interested in my own body, and like something I should keep a secret. But it also feels empowering to be learning the intricate details that will help me get pregnant. I track my sleep patterns, sexual arousal, and cervical mucous for colour and consistency (the least intriguing part). My basal thermometer makes a reappearance on my night-stand, and I diligently check and record my temperature before I get out of bed each morning. I am learning to pay attention to the body I live in. I realize that knowledge *is* power and that I don't *need* to go to the fertility clinic to get pregnant. I've done the tests already — blood, hormone levels, ultrasound — and they all check out fine. I feel connected to the centuries of women who have charted rhythms and the moon, loved and honoured their bodies, and who have conceived.

There is one unpleasant shadow to my joy that elbows its way to the forefront of my consciousness. I have been speaking with another man about the possibility of sperm donation. Finding you means I must summon my courage to tell him what I've been feeling and dodging for a while: he is not the one. The feeling in my gut tells me so, although I can't articulate a good reason. He *almost* is. But almost is not good enough when the creation of a life (and a lifetime connection for me) is at stake. I feel like a destroyer of dreams. I see the steel of self-preservation rise as I tell him, and he wishes me well. Hope is sucked out of the space between us. I feel a contradiction of emotions — sorry for the pain my truth has caused him, and liberated by speaking my truth.

By the time I met you I had revised my sperm donor criteria so many times, my list was becoming unmanageable. Somewhere along the way my simple desire — a man of colour that I like, respect, and admire — became not good enough. Suddenly I wanted someone who spoke Spanish, someone smart and creative, environmental, spiritual, aware. My gay male friends insisted I add good looking. Between the three candidates I had, the list was complete. But for all, there was one major piece missing — the feeling that a friend calls the "full body yes." When I met you, my whole body said to me, "That's him!" No list, no criteria — no information at all. It was not a decision I made with my head, it was a command from the core of my being.

I finally tell my parents. Their reaction is anticlimactic and speaks to how foreign this must be for them. Even more than it is for me. This is not the way I had imagined conceiving and raising a child. First, there is no boyfriend to present to my parents, no physical co-creation with someone I love and curl up with at night.

My queerness has taken care of that. But now there is also no relationship to accompany this miracle, no one to talk to my belly and eventually listen with me for the patter of little feet in the morning. Sperm donation and single parenthood were not in my plan, but I have entertained the conventional alternative, and this feels more respectful of who I am in the world. It has taken me a long time to embrace my queerness; I love men, but have a love, passion, connection, and desire for women that is unequivocal. I once thought creating a family "traditionally" was more important and that I could live without the rest. I found out the hard way, and with a lot of pain, that I was wrong. After my "announcement," my mother makes some of the requisite clucks and overtures: *Who is he? What's he like? When can I meet him?* I'm embarrassed that I don't know much except what you do, where you are from, and that this feels right. The subject soon changes. Two and a half weeks of waiting to tell them the big news evaporates into the summer afternoon.

I tell a few friends — a careful selection after my experience with my parents. I choose the ones who know my journey and whom I think will share my joy, will know what this means to me — this knowing, and having found you.

I begin a two-week cleanse in preparation for pregnancy. Although I have been on cleansing diets before, this time it's not so daunting. I'm doing it for someone else's benefit. I'm preparing the baby house! I am amazed at the ease with which I have transitioned from dream to reality, from longing to planning. Preparing and nurturing my body in preparation for the child that will soon grow there feels like the most natural thing in the world to me. I feel different already: more grown up, more "on purpose."

Last week we met at your apartment to start talking about the details. We sat on your couch together and tentatively made our way through foreign territory: did you want to be part of the pregnancy? How often did you want to be present in the child's life? You brought up custody should anything happen to me, and I joked that you were killing me off already. We laughed. Having no map, it was a random mixture of imminent and future considerations. I floated to the subway afterwards, thinking about how easy it had been to talk with you, what an awesome journey this was, and how lucky I felt. Your email that night was lovely; you were feeling the same awe and excitement. I smiled to see that you also seemed to need time to sit with how you felt before expressing it. Having just been at your place, I could picture you writing the email. I marveled again at the importance of trusting my instincts. I was feeling blessed.

Today, you are coming to my home. My dog and I have walked to meet you at the streetcar, and we will continue our conversation. But before we do, before we arrive at my door, you suddenly, urgently, interrupt my nervous small talk. I feel your energy shift before you speak. "I'm having second thoughts," you blurt out, stopping us both in our tracks. I am suddenly, acutely, aware of my surroundings. Everything is in sharper focus, and I feel like I'm shrinking. It is sunny and you are wearing sunglasses, so I can't see your eyes. I suddenly feel disconnected, alone, lost. My body registers what you have said, and I gasp. I feel the ground shift under me, and I want to reach out and grab your arm, but I can't touch you. I have a sudden urge to laugh — the truth of this too devastating to contemplate. *Not now,* I hear in my head. *We're just getting started, not NOW!* I'm searching your face for the smile that will tell me you are joking. You aren't. In that moment, the bond I feel with you is broken. I see you standing in front of me, but you are a stranger. One sentence, and I feel completely and utterly alone. Sounds stop. I hear nothing except the rush of disbelief.

You are talking, still with the sunglasses on, so I can't read your eyes. You want to respect my space, so you give me the option of talking here in the park. My response is an internal mixture of politeness and incredulity. *Are you kidding? Of course we're going to my place, you've come all this way.* And *I want to be in my own space for what comes next, so I have somewhere safe to fall apart.* "No," I say, and we resume our walk.

Somehow my legs move and we arrive at my home. I feel the heady energy that means my heart is pushing away the feelings that threaten to overwhelm me, and is preparing the fortress. I don't sit beside you on the patio bench. I choose a chair so I can face you. It's an act, a clever strategy of defence. It's all I've got. I feel nauseous. I want to scream.

My life feels like it's over. Every ounce of joy I have felt has drained out of my body, and I have nothing left. I want to die. The movie playing in my head has me crumbled on the floor, unashamed, sobbing uncontrollably, a "Nooooo" escaping from my lips. *This can't be happening!* I think. *Tell me this isn't happening! There's a mistake! Oh my God!*

In real time, however, I'm sitting quietly, silently talking down the lump in my throat so the tears won't come. I've seen the movie. If I start to cry now, it may never end, and I'll dissolve into a pathetic mess.

Instead, I wait. You try to explain but stumble over words that don't begin to reach the space your declaration has blown open in me. I can tell this is hard for you. I feel your struggle and understand the challenge of being confined to words to explain something that you feel. I remember the excruciating knowledge of the link between one person's truth and another's pain. I understand. I know what it is like to be in your place. I hear the word "timing." I hear that there is a lot going on for you, and this is changing everything already. *No shit,* I want to say, *We're planning a baby! And, by the way, YOUR life isn't going to change all that much!* My wiser self knows better, understands that this is big for both of us. And then I hear it — "Something doesn't feel right" — and I know there is nothing to say. My spirit turns its back and shuts the door. Although I try, I can't argue with a feeling. It is yours.

I am bathed in grief. Thirty-eight is not an age that leaves me much in the way of leisurely baby-making time. And yet, with whom I do this is more important to me than when. I am not able to find the words to express this thought, or many others. I trip over a few attempts. I try silence, but that doesn't feel good either. Screaming probably would help, but it's out of the question. I want to cry, but I will not. I am aware of the danger here: that my devastation will make me beg; that I will push when reality is speaking so clearly and demanding I listen; that I will bulldoze through, say or do anything not to lose this dream. I understand the danger of clutching tightly to what is so close now, not accepting what you are saying, and wanting to make it better — possibly at my own expense. Something tells me not to push — wisdom or fear, I'm not sure which.

I am aware of how I want to become intellectual and spit out something smart and cold because it's easier than sharing how I feel. I tell you this, and then say, "Everything always works out as it should." I can't help it — and I do happen to believe it. " 'What can I do to help you feel better about this?' is what I really want to say," I tell you. This feels better.

I am grateful that you can tell me how you feel. I am grateful that you care enough about me not to ride your unease until later and then speak up — pretending everything is fine and that you are comfortable when you are not. I see the beauty of your honesty as I'm willing myself not to cry. "What can I do for you?" you ask. "Promise me you'll tell me if you change your mind," I say. You promise.

We have lunch. Despite everything, it feels good to have you here, and it feels easy, like we have been together for a long time and know each other's rhythm. You light the barbecue while I make the salad. We laugh together, talk about our families. We are getting to know each other. I realize that perhaps this new place with more time and less pressure gives us more freedom to do just that, while the bitter irony of it all rings in my ears.

The afternoon passes. We walk the dog together in the direction you need to go. In these past hours, I have realized how little time you have had to prepare for the enormity of this journey. I have had two and a half years to think, to dream, to plan, to imagine. Your "yes" catapulted me into action. My horse is out of the gates and at the finish line, and yours is still in the barn getting saddled. I am sorry and see how unfair — albeit exciting — this must be for you. You tell me I don't need to apologize, but the magnitude of the imbalance unsettles me.

I could walk with you for hours. It feels comfortable just being in your presence, and I don't want this journey we have started to end. I'm not ready. It's been too short. But I pick a place to turn back, conscious of the distance I will have to walk back with the dog, and the cowardice that keeps me moving, saying *one more block* in my head each time we come to a corner. Being brave would mean asking you: "What happens now? What do I do NOW? What does this mean for you and me?" At each intersection, I fool myself into thinking I'll speak up by the next one. Too soon, we are at my turning-back point.

I feel a familiar panic rising in me. My feet are tingling. I feel light-headed. I want to run. *STAY!* I want to say. *Don't go.* I want to clutch your arm and beg you not to do this. If you leave now, everything ends. I will reach down into myself and say something so moving, so real ... although not even in my fantasy can I come up with what it is I need to say to change your mind. What I do say is, "So ... I guess I'll see you around." Damn. The storm windows to my heart slam shut so automatically it scares me. I can hear myself, and I want to take the words back the minute they are out, although the weakness in the alternative plea of "Will I see you again?" makes me cringe. "We'll keep in touch," you say. "If that's okay with you." And from within my armour of self-protection I hear myself say, "Sure, abso-slutely." I berate myself for the stupidity of this word while I try to remember the cartoon character who says it — anything to distract myself. This exchange is not how I want this day to end ... this is not my truth. But I'm not in control anymore. Self-protection has taken over the wheel, and it is safety first. I can't hear another "no" from you. No more pain today.

There is no kiss on each cheek this time. Instead we hug for what seems like a long time. We haven't been this physically close before. It feels like a mixture of things I can't put my finger on: comfort, reassurance, regret, good-bye and hello. I feel your hand on my back for the first time. It is a closer hug than the others; something seems to hold us together. Perhaps we are bound by shared loss and a new level of vulnerability.

You walk east and I walk west towards home. I look back once. My dog is tired so it takes us a long time to walk back. I alternate between the feeling in my stomach that warns me there isn't much time to get home before I start to cry, and the acknowledgment that "not now" does not mean "no," that with whom I do this, and how it feels, are more important to me than when. I know I need to trust that time will reveal the gift that this turn of events holds for both of us.

When I am safe at home, in my bedroom, I begin to write on the pages next to last week's joy. I cannot. A deep and sudden scribble marks the page instead, tearing the paper. I dial a number. When I hear a familiar "hello," I ask my friend how she is doing and if she has time to talk to me for a few minutes. She hears something in my voice and leaves her peach cobbler for a quiet room. "I'm going to be fine," I say. "I just need to cry with someone for a bit." These words, true or not, help the tears come more than telling the story, which I can't do for minutes as my devastation finally washes over the levees of bravery I've built during the last six hours. I am surprised by the force with which my sobs grip me, even with a witness. There are no words for the depth of disappointment I feel, but I say enough so she understands. She says all the right things, I stop crying, and we hang up.

But I am not done yet. The ugly cry comes next. The crying we do alone so no one hears, the wailing that starts in the belly and makes its way up through every crevice and space in our being, collecting force and rage along the way. It is the type of crying that requires I get as close to the ground as possible. I want to crawl. I am trying to ground myself so I don't tear open.

I don't know what to do with myself after this. I pace around my small home in circles. There is no one I feel like calling, except you. Now that there is physical distance I feel safe enough to reveal my pain. I want to ask you why, and what happened? Instead, I find some work to do. It saves me from this certain mistake, but every time the phone rings I hope it's you, calling to talk, to talk it over. Finally, I sit down and write it all down, spilling my emotion onto paper. Eventually, I go to bed.

At four a.m. I am awake. The three a.m. time of grieving has passed and the anger has arrived. The biting words keep me company for a little while, and I continue to write by hand in pencil.

When I'm done, the sadness creeps in, and I cry into my pillow. Curling around it for comfort, I fall asleep again. I have a dream. In my dream the front of my condo is made entirely of glass. Like a motel, there is a balcony that connects me to my neighbours. A woman stands outside against the railing. She asks how I am. "I am okay," I tell her. "No matter where I am — and I've done some pretty stupid things — someone is watching over me."

"And how do you pray?" she asks me.

"That is a personal question," I say. "Come over here." She does.

"Sometimes it's random and erratic," I say.

"I can help you with that," she answers.

"Sometimes it's fervent," I say. "Sometimes it's just two words over and over: help me, help me, help me, help me …."

I wake up. My body is tingling, and I feel grounded and connected. I wonder for a moment if yesterday really happened, and then the lurch in my belly reminds me it was real. The remnants of my dream surround me like a shawl, and I feel held.

Dirty Rotten Egg

By Dawn Whitwell

On July 12, 2004, my dear friend took me out for dinner and asked me to be her egg donor. It was the most exciting thing anyone had ever asked me to do. My dear friend, hereinafter referred to as the Recipient, and her husband, hereinafter referred to as the Spouse, hereinafter referred to collectively as the Intended Parents (IPs), and I, hereinafter referred to as the Donor, were giddy imagining the future.

The IPs loved my immediate reaction — which was "YES!" — since they had researched such things and found that exuberant "yeses" were the best possible response when proposing to your donor. And the synchronicities didn't begin there. When they first learned they could use a known donor, they were in separate cities and both said my name almost at the same time.

All my life I have been obsessed with people's families. Even as a kid I needed to know what made a family. Why was ours the only house that looked like a Hells Angels convention when we had family over? I was sure something was going on in the other houses in our neighbourhood, that they were doing everything the same, and that my family alone was doing everything different. And my mom might be doing it on purpose.

So I started conducting my own field research. We lived in a new neighbourhood; some of the houses didn't even have grass yet. As new families moved in, I began knocking on their doors. I would say, "Do you have kids?" and "Can I come in anyway?" and "Were you in any wars?" I wanted to observe other families, to know what kind of socks they wore and how mad their moms got. One Sunday I sat with a different family at church. Just strangers. I just stopped following my family and ducked into a row at the back. They knew who I was: the one with the two sisters and the single mom who always sat in the front row. I went up for communion and walked right past my mother in the front pew, on her knees, the Lord stuck to the roof of her mouth.

"Dawn Marie!" she hissed in as loud a whisper as she could manage. "Get back here!" I kept walking, back up to my new stranger family, half smiling at the thought of my mother interrupting a sacrament to yell at me. I would use that against her in the car.

It didn't help that my mother dismissed my questions, explaining that she couldn't be expected to know anything because of how she was so young when she had me. I would grill her to no avail.

"Am I adopted? Are you sure you took the right baby home from the hospital? Did I have a twin that you had to give away because you and Dad were poor?"

So you can understand my reaction, my absolute "YES!" when the IPs asked me to be their donor.

I could watch a version of myself grow up with a family I would choose. "YES!"

A fucking do-over? "YES!"

Tests? "Fine." Surgery? "No probs." Lots of appointments? "Of course!" Hormones, fertility drugs, other medical risks? "I'm honoured to be chosen, incredibly favoured by chance." "Yeah, generous, I know, but it's a gift to me too."

The whole world turned into APPLAUSE signs. All three of us — me and the IPs — were stunned by our collective simpatico. There were so many cherries on top of this sundae, one of which was that my wife and I didn't want to have our own kids. We had decided it was too hard. We love babies, and would love to recognize our child's divine essence as one and the same as our own, but after witnessing our many friends give up sleep, sex, and movies, we decided it wasn't worth our relationship. Also, we mused, having a baby would make it difficult for each of us to start dating again.

I would be an aunt to the IPs' child, and I rule at being an aunt. The IPs and I relentlessly imagined how this all might play out, which the in vitro fertilization people tell you not to do, and then make you do in several controlled settings, as if one can control it. I began to fantasize over the potential of my DNA, which made me feel like an idiot. In retrospect, though, it was impossible not to.

When I was being screened medically, I was asked to imagine giving myself daily, sometimes twice-daily, hormone injections, accompanied by blood draws, and the egg retrieval process. I was also asked to imagine my genetic history, what this child would inherit from me and my ancestors.

During psychological screening, I was asked to imagine endless scenarios of my future with my new family. What if I had children that weren't as good as the child I gave to them? What if they had an abortion? What if the child was retarded? What if I disagreed with how they raised the child? In the case of the IPs' accidental, unfortunate, and simultaneous death, would I want custody of the child?

At every stage of screening I was told how generous I was, what an incredible gift I was giving my friends. My Recipient also started showering me with gifts. Every time she picked me up for an appointment, almost daily, she presented me with an unnecessary present. On these drives to and from the clinic, it was impossible not to enter the danger zone by talking about it, all of it: what the IPs' families thought, what my family thought. We decided to tell only a few close friends and family, until the baby was born. Then we would tell the world and toast to friendship! The few friends I told were ecstatic, envious — and who could blame them?

My Recipient and I trotted on our giddy horses to the mandatory information session on IVF that the clinic ran. It was one thing we could do while we waited to begin a cycle. She had already been to a session and insisted I didn't need to pay attention. We wrote notes to each other instead. "I wish they hadn't said it was up to a higher power," she wrote to me. I wrote back: "Do you think we look like a lesbian couple?" We did. She came back with some lab gossip: "I heard this guy watches over the embryos like they're his own." I wondered in my next note: "Where do they get their porn?" "Maybe the nurse has to go buy it," she responded.

A month in, my Recipient and I started on the birth control pill. Our cycles had to synch before I could start the IVF protocol.

We waited. A lot. For my period to arrive, to synch up with my Recipient's, to start another cycle. It's funny whom I started to envy while waiting. Chickens ovulate almost every day. The first time that a needle left a bruise, I remember thinking, "Good!" I was glad to have something to show for all the early-morning ultrasounds, for all my thoughts, and all the needles that didn't leave a mark.

A month later, I began with injections. That cycle was canceled around week five because I wasn't responding well to the drugs. "Not to worry," we were told: another protocol would suit me better. It took another two months before we were synched to Cycle 2. By then, we were less giddy.

Four weeks into the second protocol, on my Recipient's birthday, we were told it wouldn't work. She and I fought tears as the doctor explained to me that I had premature ovarian failure. I had failed to produce enough ova. There would be no more cycles. In fact, they recommended that if I wanted to have a baby, *I* should use an egg donor. Thanks.

I bought my Recipient a birthday lunch after the appointment, and gave her shattered dreams. We were stunned and silent. The Spouse called for the bad news and told the Recipient to send his love to me. My Intended Parents were sorry for me, that I'd received bad news out of all of it. I was sorry for me, for not getting to procreate ... with them.

So I was not selected. Or favoured by chance. It felt like I had been dumped by evolution. I had gone from being naturally selected, literally, to watching myself be selected out. Unnecessary for the survival or adaptation of the human species. Apparently our species doesn't need anymore depressed, smart-ass genes who can't make small talk. I had been dumped before, but not on this scale.

To make things worse, I seemed to be surrounded by examples

of reproductive success. It seemed like all my friends became pregnant at the same time. I remember being stunned by the number of redheads in the world. Isn't that a recessive trait? I learned that desert locust eggs can remain in the ground for 20 years, all waiting for the same rainstorm to hatch. Plagues were more necessary than me.

In my denial, I rationalized that I had evolved from cats anyway. That's where I get my binge-eating survival gene. And my napping-all-afternoon gene. If a cat and a glacier could mate, I figured, they would make me. And I would be visible from space.

My Former Intended Parents turned immediately to an anonymous donor, and I turned to embracing everything and anything that parents couldn't do. Like baking French pastry all night, high, then eating it at five a.m. Real French pastry, like from a French recipe. In French. From France. I don't speak French, but my wife, hereinafter referred to as Wonderwall, does, so I videotaped it and tried to get her to take her top off the whole time.

I played the whole nine months of being an "egg donor" over and over in my mind, trying to figure it out. How could something so perfect not be? My Former IPs had moved on, but I didn't know how to. There are no failed donor support groups. In my depressed stupor, I rationalized that breeding was unoriginal.

Meanwhile, I had agreed to act as labour support for my Former Recipient while the Former Spouse was out of town. The Former Recipient got me a cell phone in case the shit went down. I carried it everywhere, checked it often. I took my role very seriously, trying to make up for being dead inside.

Then the cell phone rang.

My Former IPs looked up when I ran into the labour room. "We're so happy you're here!" they told me. It seemed like the birth would never happen, like my Former Recipient would just be in agony for the rest of her life. Then, it happened so fast. Then, there he was. All folded up. Former Spouse — hereinafter referred to as Daddy — and I held up Former Recipient's — hereinafter known as Mommy's — hands so she could take the wet little prince from the doctors. She was so delirious, for a moment she didn't know what or whom she was taking until she knew and was so happy. She cried like Holly Hunter in *Raising Arizona:* "I love him so much!"

And I felt chosen again, and favoured by chance. Honoured to witness his crowning. Prince of the-universe-finally-coming-together. Prince of all gentle things.

That prince is almost two, and I have a very special place in his life, and he in mine. He is the closure, the "reason" something so seemingly and seamlessly perfect didn't work. I've only imagined it the other way once, that my DNA were part of him.

It wasn't as good.

It Ain't a Rough Patch, Baby

By Diane Flacks

When my partner and I initially talked about having a baby, every option was on the table, including anonymous sperm donation. And it was an attractive, relatively sterile, no-strings-attached centrepiece. Friends who went that way were happy with their decision, and were admittedly conscious that they wanted to be parents without interference.

Then we met a lesbian couple, their two kids (then seven and four) and their known donor/Daddy. It was a Sunday, and they were all having brunch together. It was a civilized, warm, mature gathering. They looked at their kids' artwork, tried to get them to eat more than cookies, and the moms asked the donor-dad to please not give them gum. They mentioned that they'd had a "rough patch" at the beginning of their parenting relationship but now felt like they were all benefiting. They could barely remember what the "rough patch" was about — something to do with the non-bio mom's legal status. But now, there was clarity and respect. And scones.

We thought, "This looks gooood!"

I was viscerally attracted to the idea that a child conceived with a known donor would know his or her biological heritage, intimately. We had dreams of openness, inclusion, and security.

We were equally adamant that we didn't want or need a coparent. My partner and I would be fully legally and financially responsible. We'd be in charge of all decisions, and we'd consult our donor on major ones. Our donor would have regular, scheduled time with our child. On paper, it looked pretty simple.

My attraction to the mysterious realm of "going known" surprised me. Generally, I'm pretty fearful, and somewhat easily threatened, and here I was, wanting to bring someone else into my family. In a pretty indefinable role. With whom I was not in love. For life.

However, once I jumped on board it felt like an adventure in frontier life-creation. We were going to do this our way, a new way. No forms to fill out, no money changed hands; we didn't even have to leave our house!

Originally my partner planned to get pregnant. I was going to be the cheerleader: "Knock her up! Get her up! Waaaaay up!" But after 18 months of unsuccessful attempts, we knew we had to choose another path. Me.

Our donor, DaddyDonor1 (DD1), was fully game. So after a short break, it was my turn. It took two tries.

When our son Eli was born, and we were awash in the undertow of new parenthood, we went through our "rough patch." Don't get me wrong: we were in bliss. And I was challenged to my core. Becoming first-time parents is straining and difficult in the best of times — I've never fought so ferociously with my partner. But add to that negotiating a third party's involvement when there are few role models to look to. It may throw you for a loop — when you're already loopy on hormones.

I decided that if anyone ever asked me about using a known donor I would be honest: It ain't a "rough patch." More like: "a long, winding trail that requires great caution because *you* are blazing it; it's barely lit, and you will be very, very tired. Try to remember to be both direct and kind."

(And while we're all about being honest, let me say this: Sure, my post-baby body looks the same as before ... in *clothes*.)

Here is a quick top four tips — learned both from personal and anecdotal experience as we travel over, under, and above the rough patches:

1) When that first baby comes, you will be exhausted and need space and time alone to bond as a new family. Take it. It won't come again.

2) While creating a document that outlines details of the known-donor arrangement is crucial, I wouldn't waste time or money hammering out donor agreements through lawyers. They're truly not worth the paper they're printed on. However, we live in an enlightened country — a leader in human rights of which we can be proud. There are concrete legal protections available to the non-bio mom. She can adopt, you can create a custody agreement through the courts, and/or you can put both moms' names on the birth certificate. I know putting two moms on the birth certificate is not supposed to apply to known-donation, but what the fuck.

3) Listening and talking can never be overrated, but you may have to be sensitive to everyone's different communication styles. A good friend once said to me, "You know how terrible you feel when you can't talk about something that's really upsetting you? That's how some men feel when they *have* to talk about things." Ideally, all parties will model good communication for your children.

4) This parenting arrangement is for life. With luck, you'll be at each other's funerals. Which is a great incentive to make this work.

A confession: I did not have a handle on most of these things until after we had our second son.

A friend once told me that becoming parents to a second child may be exponentially more work, but it's also much easier than becoming a parent the first time. The first time, you change irrevocably, shockingly, totally. You suddenly find yourself with anxieties reminiscent of your mother's, singing mindless songs in a baby group, with spit-up epaulettes on each of your shoulders.

When it came time to consider a second child, we were torn. After a difficult pregnancy and dangerous childbirth, I did not think

I could do it again.

So my partner decided to see if it was possible for her to get pregnant. The window was closing and she didn't know if she could, but she needed to try.

She decided to immediately ask for help from a fertility clinic. They discovered that there was a problem. The problem was there was no problem. Tests indicated that there was no reason she could not be pregnant. Her doctor hypothesized that maybe she and DD1 just weren't a "good fit." This mysterious phenomenon occurs sometimes with straight couples, too. The male's sperm and female's eggs just aren't compatible. With this information, we decided not to waste another 18 months. There was no time to lose. My partner was 39.

Enter DD2: an old friend of my partner's who'd been working in China for years and had been someone she'd originally contemplated as a donor.

Negotiating the terms of our parenting arrangement with DD1 was a slow, thoughtful process. With DD2, it was quicker. But that was *not* because of the old adage, "when you have your first child and their pacifier drops on the ground, you boil it and sterilize it before giving it back to your baby. By the second child, you wipe it on the dog."

It was not because we cared less or were too exhausted. It was quicker because we were wiser. We'd been parents already. We knew our bottom lines — both for ourselves, and for our child.

One of the things DD2 said was that he wouldn't want to have much to do with a baby in the first two years. And then he'd be happy to have weekly access, similar to DD1's.

But I knew how it would go. I said to DD2, "*When* you want to see the baby regularly in the first two years, and you *will*, just go through me." I suggested this because I knew it was inevitable, and because it was fine with my partner and me.

We began insemination on our own while waiting for the clinic and the sperm bank to be ready to help us proceed. At home, unassisted medically, my partner got pregnant on the second try. We were stunned. We didn't really think it would happen for her, and certainly not so fast! We decided not to tell anyone until three months had passed.

At our 13-week ultrasound, all seemed fine. So, we told our eldest son that Mommy was going to have a baby, and that his brother or sister had his or her *own* donor, his or her *own* Dad.

"Okay," Eli said, inscrutably. We asked him what he wanted to call the baby in Mommy's womb. He said, "Raspberry." And informed us that it was a girl.

DD1 asked a really good question. "What will he or she call me?... Uncle?" We shrugged. We knew of no model for this.

By week 20 of my partner's pregnancy we had discovered that our baby was going to be born with two serious medical conditions that would require surgery and lengthy hospitalization in the first year of his life.

Jonathan was born, and life became about veering from crisis to crisis. There was no time for complex interpersonal issues. We hunkered down and took it day by day, moment by moment.

While Jonathan was in hospital, DD2 came by once a week to spend time alone in the NICU with him. He was smitten the moment he saw him in his warming crib. We suggested a weekly visit, which would allow my partner and me to both be at home for some precious dinner hours with our elder son. DD2 immediately agreed. In Jonny's room there were three other babies. Often either Jonny or another baby would be in extreme distress, in critical condition. Some babies died. This was not what DD2 signed up for. But he never blinked.

DD1 was extremely helpful in keeping Eli's spirits up and normalizing life for him. He was a crucial support. He adores Jonny — and navigates this uncharted landscape with grace, humour, and enormous love and generosity. It's beautiful to see.

For the first year of Jonathan's life, Eli had to weather a pseudo sibling. A brother who existed, but lived in the isolated, forbidding world of the hospital, whom he could visit for short periods of time, a few days a week.

Finally, when Jonathan came home, he was delicate and required special care.

I was once reading an Arthur book to Eli wherein Arthur is jealous of his new baby sister. I asked Eli if he ever felt that way about Jonathan or that Jonathan was getting too much of our attention. "But Mama," he said, "you never give Jonny more attention than me. I always get lots of attention."

Bingo.

We may have made mistakes in this journey. We know we'll have challenges to come — whether it's with two DDs, or with a child with two rare medical conditions, or with another who is incredibly smart and high energy, or with two moms who are tired and busy and need more time together. There won't be many people to turn to for guidance.

One thing I've learned, though, is that the road ahead is completely unknown for everyone. Anything can happen. You can plan the most traditional, conservative, normative parenting paradigm, and it can all get shot to hell.

For myself, I can only do what I do best — mother our children.

And, as I did a few days ago, learn from them.

When I picked Eli up from Grade One the other day, he informed me that the kids had to all write in their journal what was special about them. He told me one of his answers about himself and then said he went back and wrote a second answer. "I'm special because I have three parents." Then he asked if we could go get a chocolate croissant.

In that moment, I was humbly reminded that, amid all the delicate complexity, the semantics of the words "dad" and "parent," the efforts to understand one another and be compassionate, on some levels it is "that simple." And that this is what we do it all for. For our children to viscerally understand how special they are.

Now, here we are, six years after we began, with a six- and a two-year-old, all hanging out at Halloween, with warmth, love, respect, civility, and comfort. With feelings of family I could not have imagined possible. With children who are loved unconditionally from all angles, with secure boundaries, and roles that are clear.

Both men are devoted to their sons, and they are delighted by and inclusive of their sons' brothers. I guess what we call them is "family."

The Spawn, the Spawnlet,
and the Birth of a Queer Family

BY TORSTEN BERNHARDT, MARCIE GIBSON,
ERIN SANDILANDS, JAKE SZAMOSI, AND ANDREA ZANIN

Part 1: The Spawn
Andrea

I was never quite sure of my place in the story you're about to read, and at times I wondered if I really had one. Nowadays, years after it all began, I think that if I had to name my role, it would be that of witness. I've been the asker of questions, the repository of stories, the observer of situations, the provider of context, the one who stands by and watches as things progress, and who remembers, and records. And as we've worked to write this piece all together, I'm finding that my latest role as compiler and editor is a natural extension of all that. Sure, I've held the position of friend, partner, ex, spaunty, lover, babysitter, movie date and more, but right now I'll be your story weaver. Pleased to meet you.

Allow me to introduce you to the main characters in this story. First and foremost, we have Marcie and Erin, the dyke couple who, sometime in 2002, decided they wanted to make a baby. They're a gorgeous pair, both of them pleasantly bespectacled and very well-spoken. Marcie's got fine features, pale skin, shoulder-length dark hair, and a penchant for overalls and striped socks. She tends to be deliberate in her movements and kind in her tone. Erin stands an impressive six feet tall, and is slim of build, with wide, intelligent eyes, olive skin, short brown hair, and boundless enthusiasm. Marcie, at the time, was a community organizer for a small not-for-profit and a crisis intervention worker with the Montreal Sexual Assault Centre, and was heavily involved with the United Church of Canada. Erin was just beginning med school, having worked as a drama therapist.

Of course, when two women want to have a kid, that's the beginning of an adventure that often involves a whole community of people. One of those people was Jake, whom I'd met in 2001. At the time it all began, Jake was a precocious genderqueer linguistics student at McGill University. Short and huggable, with long, dark hair and a remarkable ability to intelligently debate just about any point for days, Jake was dating Torsten, whom I'd met in 2000. Torsten's a tall and lanky guy who, despite his square German jaw and pronounced nose, somehow manages to pull off a gentle, long-haired, queer-boy vibe. Maybe it's his sheer geekiness — he is, after all, a freelance biological illustrator, museum generalist, and computer programmer. Or maybe it's that almost all his partners have been dykes or trans people.

The story includes other characters, too, in a multi-layered web of connection that I'll try to explain as we go. There are Bear and J, a wonderful pair of trans guys who are both writers, speakers, and activists working to make the world a better place for trans and queer people; there's Dave, a soft-spoken queer bio-guy who studies math and gives the gentlest back rubs. There's Helen, a red-headed cello player who's a social worker by day and a queer swing dancer by night. There's Mitch, a sweet trans fairy boi and high school teacher, and Linz, a cocky, butch dyke logistics officer and soccer player. In truth, the whole cast is even more extensive than that, but we are writing an essay, after all, not an epic play.

As for me, my name's Andrea, and I'm a freelance writer and editor, and a happily polyamorous queer. I also write and teach about all sorts of alternative forms of sexuality — kink, non-monogamy, GLBT issues, and more. Now, it appears, I write about queer family too.

In any case, Jake started dating Torsten in late 2001, and met Erin and Marcie through their mutual friend Maïda in early 2002. As Marcie and Erin extended their search for a sperm donor in 2003, Jake put them in touch with Torsten ... and the rest, as they say, is history.

Jake and Torsten eventually split up, and Jake moved to Toronto for a time. A few months after that, in early 2004, Torsten and I began our relationship. When he and I started seeing each other, Torsten had just entered the process of sperm donation. Because dykes are generally linked by two degrees of separation or less, I had met Marcie and Erin years before when they attended a couple of events I organized with a queer women's group in Montreal. I'd always thought they were nice, but we hadn't really gotten to know one another ... and all of a sudden, my partner was fertilizing their eggs. It created an odd sort of intimacy among relative strangers. The process had its amusing moments; there were, among other things, some odd restrictions on my sex life with Torsten, since on certain days he needed to save his sperm for Marcie. This presented no particular issue for me — as a committed non-monogamist and as a woman who didn't (and still doesn't) want children of her own, I certainly felt no claim of ownership over Torsten's seed, and I was excited by the prospect of seeing a new queer family form before my very eyes.

Now, I kind of expected to stand by on the sidelines and cheer, and perhaps send a congratulatory card when the Spawn (as we so elegantly nicknamed the unborn child) finally popped out to greet the world. But somewhere in there, Marcie and Erin began to involve me in the process. It was subtle at first — the occasional dinner date, the warm conversations, the hugs. I'm not really sure when I started to feel like I was actually a part of the story rather than an occasional reader, but I do remember feeling a dawning sense of tenderness and gratitude toward the whole process and everyone involved. When Marcie's brother Geoff coined the term "spuncle" to explain Torsten's avuncular role in the sperm-donation process, and happily crowned me "spaunty," I just about cried. I've always valued family, the intentional kind all the more so, but I never expected to be adopted into such a beautiful one by virtue of simply being there to watch it. The birth of Eli happened on January 31, 2005, but over the year before, a whole family gestated and was quietly born too.

Jake

I don't know if my co-authors are aware of this, but I was against it. When I was first asked if I thought Torsten would be willing to be a sperm donor, I was casually excited in a "yay-queer-baby!" sort of way. But once I'd passed the message on, and we started talking about it for real, I had some serious reservations. At the time, I was looking at the possibility of a lifetime with Torsten, and while I understood that he would be signing away all legal rights and responsibilities, I doubted that that would be the end of it. I mean, all the paperwork in the world wouldn't stop the future child from just showing up and expecting a relationship, and I hadn't even met the kid yet. How was I supposed to deal with that? I felt way too young. So we talked about it for quite some time, on and off, and I would try to lead him away from doing it, but by the time we broke up a few months later, he still hadn't made a decision, and that was fine with me.

I wasn't really around much during the time that Marcie was trying to conceive. I saw Erin and Marcie only very occasionally. I had heard that Torsten had agreed and that they were trying and, even though I was no longer directly affected by the decision, I was concerned. What about Torsten? I knew well how much he didn't want to be a parent, and you can't control a kid, you know? God only knew what it was going to want from Torsten as it grew up, and how was Torsten going to deal with that? It was no longer my business, so I kept my mouth shut, but I just thought it was a bad idea.

Then I had to move to Toronto for a while and by the time I got back to Montreal, Marcie was eight months' pregnant, and I was starting to warm to the idea. Don't get me wrong, I was still worried. But it's hard not to be excited about a baby.

By this time I was dating Dave, who was soon to become Torsten's roommate. Torsten and I were thus able to maintain our connection; as a bonus, I was able to become closer with Andrea.

And then Eli was born. And when I met him and realized that without me he wouldn't even be here, all my doubts just disap-peared. He was the most perfect baby. How could I ever have worried or thought that this could possibly be a bad idea? I had been so scared, and the memory almost baffles me now.

Marcie and Erin

Like most creative projects, the process of creating Eli took us a long way from where we had imagined it would. In 2002, we were a pair of queer girls with a couple of cats, occasional weekend foster kids, and a lot of free time. We decided that we needed goals, projects that would be fulfilling and engaging. Erin decided she wanted to be a doctor. Marcie decided she wanted to be pregnant and try parenting from scratch. We each thought the other was crazy.

"Just finish the arts degree," Marcie begged. "Get out of school and move on."

Erin looked at her quizzically. "You're a lesbian," she reasoned, "and pregnancy gives people hemmorhoids, and nausea, and prolapsed bladders. Let's just start fostering kids full-time."

But we plowed ahead: Marcie supported Erin through a math course for folks who dropped it in tenth grade, and Erin reciprocated by helping with the search for sperm.

In lesbian relationships, pregnancy requires conversation, staging, and other people beyond a parental couple. It breaks apart the notion that the nuclear family can ever exist, has ever existed, without a wider community. We weren't trying to replicate this false model, to pretend that if we bought sperm from an anonymous source we could be "just like them — but two women." With no pretence that this would be a child made purely of discrete intimacy, we wanted this queer kid to start from queer beginnings, recognizing and telling the story of everyone involved, without the commoditization of human tissue. No closets, no secrets, no pretend, no shame.

Besides all of the above, frozen swimmers are expensive, and neither of us was employed full-time. Also, at the time, Quebec fertility clinics were still suffering from Roman Catholic hangovers that prevented them from serving lesbians and single women. The best-case scenario to achieve our goals was to find a male friend who "made his own swim team." So we made a list of all the people we knew who were likely to make sperm and to whom we could imagine popping the question.

The first person we approached was enthusiastic, but as the conversation progressed, we all realized that he really wanted to be a dad, not a donor. The second person we asked was really supportive, and we got down to the business of trying. After a few unsuccessful cycles, though, we all realized that things could become complicated. He was straight, and used to sharing his sex life with his parents in a "Mom, meet my girlfriend" kind of way. Suddenly, he was in a position where he needed to come out. Our relationship had queered him, and by extension, his bio-family — who were none too thrilled about the idea of a genetic grandchild to whom they were not "really" grandparents. We broke up.

The next guy we asked sat down for supper and said something to the effect of, "Whoa, girls, I know what you're going to ask me, and the answer is no." He had already been a donor for another couple who had two fabulous kids, but he had never told anyone about his involvement. He had great tips on the logistics of transferring sperm from one party to the other that now seem obvious in retrospect, but at the time seemed like ingenious ways to minimize the awkwardness implicit in the process. His "girls leave for a walk, then boy goes for a walk" method became the standard from then on in.

We asked another friend, who was again super, and supportive, and we tried for a cycle, but he lived six hours away and the inconvenience made it impossible to continue. For a pair of queer girls who thought we had a lot of male friends, we realized we had reached the end of our list. No sperm. We were stumped.

We started mentioning our quest to everyone we knew, throwing the net wide to see whom we might meet.

Torsten

It feels like we were all so innocent when this began. Jake mentioned offhandedly one day that his friend Maïda's friends, a lesbian couple, were looking for a sperm donor. A few weeks later we were over at Maïda's when Marcie called; when Maïda passed the phone to Jake, he spoke with Marcie for a bit and then exclaimed, "Here's Torsten, he has sperm!" and thrust the phone at me. Marcie and I spoke about the idea of donating, a little awkwardly, and decided to meet up to see how we felt. At the time I really had no idea what I was getting myself into.

When we first met, it was a little surreal. I wanted to be sure that they knew about my experience with cancer and about my family's past. For my part, I wanted to be sure that they were people that I'd be comfortable helping to have a child. If not, they could no doubt find someone else. (How hard could it be to find a donor? I thought, not knowing what they'd already gone through.)

The conversation went well, and when I got home I started to look into the legalities of the whole process. The Internet had an unsurprisingly large number of horror stories, but it seemed that as long as we used artificial insemination things would be fine. Not having any rights or responsibilities seemed pretty good to me at the time. Looking at it again, more than half a decade into the whole crazy process, it's nice that things have progressed through organic and mutual (if often unspoken) agreements rather than due to any official responsibilities.

Marcie and Erin seemed so on the ball. They had a form for all of us to sign that covered all the bases, as far as I could tell. Nothing written up by a lawyer, but it had been researched and seemed complete. They also had the whole setup for the insemination attempts worked out: we all eat brunch together, they go for a walk, I hand Marcie a container with my sperm in it when they get back and then Erin and I would make awkward conversation in the living room while Marcie did something mysterious in the bedroom. It was a strange process to be *not* having sex with Marcie, the dyke I was trying to impregnate, and then having sex with Andrea, the dyke I was trying *not* to impregnate.

The problem was that Marcie wasn't getting pregnant. I was fairly certain that my sperm was good, having gotten two women pregnant in the past while using birth control, and one of those post-chemo. It didn't bother me overly, since I still didn't have too much invested at the time, but I felt bad for them — and after a while it all started to feel ridiculous.

That said, the protracted process was a good way to get to know them better, at least. Once we found out about the wacky medical shenanigans that were necessary to kick-start Marcie into ovulating, things made a bit more sense, though the exact timing that was needed for insemination kept the surreality level at an acceptable high. But it wasn't until Marcie and Erin made a trip to the fertility clinic to look at my sperm under a microscope and make sure that all was well in Swimmerville that said sperm finally decided to get on with their raison d'être. The test showed no medical issues, but apparently the little guys wanted their 15 minutes of fame *before* they'd perform.

Marcie and Erin

We had been trying for the better part of a year with a variety of sperm, and were beginning to think that it might be worth going to see a doctor just to make sure things were on track to conceive if and when we located another donor. By that time, the law had changed, and Quebec fertility clinics were now obliged to serve women who weren't married to men. Partly in a move to open up services to us unmarried gals, a private clinic appeared on the scene.

As it happened, Marcie wasn't ovulating. No egg, no baby — even if we did find sperm. We moved from the private project of beeping bedside thermometers to the medical world of Clomid and follicle counts, hysterosalpingograms and dildocams and, "Yes, we really do need to be inseminating on Thursday at nine a.m."

We tried to make ourselves appear relaxed and un-desperate when Torsten came over for brunch-and-cup-and-syringe time. Despite spending three mornings a week fretting in a doctor's office — and spending considerable money on the gamble — we didn't want to appear too intense. We imagined the maybe-baby over Montreal bagels and fruit platters, and tried to seem comfortable about a casual exchange of semen with someone whose last name we didn't yet know when we wrote up our donor contract.

In some ways it upended our sense of the "usual" courtship. We barrelled through the get-to-know-you process, learning each other's stories and quirks at "casual" light speed while engaging in levels of discussion, intimacy, and relational ties way beyond the scope of most first dates. Of course, we weren't getting married, and there was no obligation to continue to see each other regularly beyond the goal in question. We wanted to stay in touch, but were keeping a degree of distance for legal reasons and in an effort not to scare Torsten off or corner him into something beyond that to which he had agreed. But despite the awkward and somewhat artificial beginning, the connections grew organically between us, and it got easier — or as easy as it gets for three socially awkward, shy, geeky introverts.

Coincidentally, after the post-coital test (an ironic term for it in this case) that put Torsten's sperm under the microscope and on the TV screen, Marcie got pregnant with the Spawn. There was a brief, harried six weeks of worrying that there might be four embryos (quadruplets!), and what the hell were we going to do? In fact, there were originally twins, but one miscarried during the second six weeks of pregnancy. Happily, though, our one little one stuck.

Torsten

Pregnancy went its merry way all on its own and pretty smoothly from my point of view. I felt somewhat more involved by that time, but not phenomenally so. My perspective was still largely that of an outsider.

When Eli was born, I wasn't there for several reasons, not the least of which was uncertainty on all sides about my position in everything. Another reason was that Erin and the midwife already filled both slots Marcie had for delivery-room visitors, so there was no room anyway. My official notification about Eli's birth came when Erin called me to ask if I would "like to meet a brand-new person." I bused my way over to the hospital and found the birthing centre — and finally got to welcome Eli to the world after what seemed like an eternity of trying to get him here.

Marcie and Erin

Eli's birth was beautiful. In one grand swoop he came gushing into the world and instantly looked around for what he wanted: warmth, skin, love, food. Determined, trust not faltering for a moment, that we would care for him and love him as fiercely in the world as we had when he was on the inside.

Erin has said on a number of occasions that the whole "fucking and not impregnating and impregnating but not fucking" business makes this all feel as though, while Eli has a set of practical, everyday parents, he also has Torsten, Andrea, Jake, and Dave as parents in a very queer sense; a scaffold of relationships that supported his creation. Even if we are read as a lesbian-nuclear family by straight eyes, it feels wrong to call Eli "mine" or "our" in front of any of them, as we would with other people. In any case, Eli had no trouble adjusting to the concept of queer family: of two mamas, of a spuncle and spaunty, of various uncles, of people yet unclassified but intrinsically important. It is all he has ever known.

Torsten

Was it then that the whole thing became real to me? It felt more real, definitely, but I had no idea where all this was going to go. Nor did I know what to expect, having almost no experience with babies. Seeing Eli that first time was a big step into an enormous uncertainty.

Marcie and Erin

Naming him was easy. In Quebec it is very difficult to legally change your name so we wanted to give him as many possibilities as we could think of, in case someday he didn't fit his first given name. We gave Eli Erin's last name (Sandilands) in part because we like the imagery of it, and in part to make crossing international borders easier, figuring it would make it less likely for her parental status to be questioned legally or socially. Thanks to some tireless lobbying from the Lesbian Mothers' Association in Quebec, Eli's birth certificate classifies us as "Mother" and "Mother," with no distinction and no need for a second-parent adoption process. As this was a relatively new legal option, many of the birth forms were not up to speed, but were creatively amended in the moment.

Naming ourselves was not so simple. Marcie wanted to be known as Mama, with possible appendices. Erin tried out being Dad, as it seemed to reflect the role she was playing, but the name didn't work out in practice. Marcie felt closeted by referring to "Eli's dad," and many people just didn't or wouldn't get into it. So we settled into MamaE and MamaM, and also answer these days to many other names Eli tries out on us, such as Garbage Truck, Dragon, and characters from books.

Trying to be responsible, we set about writing wills. We thought about what we would want for Eli if both of us were to die. It was important for us that he be with family who knew him and loved him, people who would value and nurture his relationships with his family/families — biological, legal, and queer. Through a tangled web of longstanding relationship, J had always been Marcie's heart, so he was an obvious choice. He knew well the diversity of people involved and could parent in the same grain as our intentions. Bear, in the process of partnering with J in 2007, has also become queerly related, and we happily extended the invitation to him as well.

Jake

Once Eli was born, I started finding more excuses to call Erin and Marcie, more reasons to get together. And the more I did that, the more I wanted to do it. We would watch TV together, share meals, garden, knit. I even invited my dad to have dinner at their apartment. And after I moved away again, Erin and Marcie's household was the only place I ever considered staying when I visited Montreal.

I don't have a name for my relationship with the little guy, and I kind of wish I did. After all, I am a causal link in the chain that led to his conception. To refer to him as "my friends' kid," or even just "my friend," doesn't seem nearly complete. But what else can I call him? There is no right word. A labmate asked me who I was knitting the blanket for and, after I stutteringly tried to explain, she just started blithely referring to him as my nephew. It sort of warms my heart every time she does it, to have my connection to him freely acknowledged and accepted, as legitimate as any blood relation. But the word still chafes a little. It's nice, but it's not accurate.

Andrea

I definitely got into being a Spaunty. When Marcie, Erin, and I spent time together in the Spawn's first months of existence — often with Torsten, occasionally without — that name helped me feel like I had a place in the story, and served as a reminder that this beautiful little being was a creature born of a multi-faceted family of which I too was a part. That family also included Jake and Dave in an odd but oddly comfortable mix, with Jake's status as Torsten's ex giving the two of us grounds on which to bond, Dave's warmth and his solid presence as Torsten's roommate setting the stage for a deeper friendship between all of us, and many a late-night conversation and shared meal à quatre cementing the whole thing. A certain domesticity developed as well, as we all shared space (and negotiated for shower time) in the Torsten-and-Dave apartment, Jake and me both being frequent overnight visitors. As a constant underpinning to all that, our unifying experience of aunt-and-unclehood made for an unexpectedly strong sense of kinship among the four of us.

It was a treat to watch the little guy grow into his very distinct personality in what seemed like no time flat. My career as a traveling sex educator was just starting to gather steam in 2005, so sometimes many weeks would go by between visits, but every time I saw Eli he would offer me a sweet hug and burble charming almost-words. Or sometimes he'd just sleep while I held him, or sit quietly while I read to him or conversed with the Mamas. From the get-go, he was a fully conscious child; when he first looked me in the eye, I could tell he was sizing me up. Luckily he judged me worthy of cuddle time. I always felt privileged when he settled comfortably in my lap, or let me spoon some food into his mouth. Those visits reminded me of watching a flower bloom on a high-speed video; every time I saw him, he was bigger, smarter, more engaged.

That year, Torsten got serious about his plans to spend a year studying biological illustration in Seattle. We intended to move there together, thinking it would be an exciting adventure; I began to step down from my community commitments and prepared to sublet my apartment. But our relationship faltered in the months preceding the move date, and come September, Torsten left to start school, alone. Not long after that, we split up.

I remember, even then, feeling that my place in this beloved queer family somehow depended on my being Torsten's partner. And so it was with some trepidation that I prepared to tell Marcie and Erin that it was over, thinking I might be saying goodbye to them — and to the Spawn too. I never thought they'd push me away; I just figured we'd gently grow apart, as people do sometimes when the connections that brought them together are severed.

It was a chilly November night when we met up for a family date at the movies during Image+Nation, Montreal's queer film festival, where we'd bought tickets to see a documentary called *QueerSpawn* — how à propos. When we found each other in the large crowd, they took in my sad face and asked what was wrong. I was still raw from the breakup, and my gut was in knots. The Mamas just held me and said kind things as I explained. The line began to move forward into the theatre, and so did we. Abruptly, Marcie turned to me and shot me a piercing look. "You're still family, you know. You're always welcome with us," she said firmly. The look of relief on my face must have spoken volumes; Erin jumped in with, "Of course!" her tone making it quite clear that any other idea would have been ludicrous. And they drew me into the theatre, and that was that.

Looking back, I realize how unfair it was for me to doubt my welcome, but at the time I was still figuring out my place in the family. In some ways, that's the night I found it. How strange that it was only upon the end of the relationship that made me a Spaunty in the first place that I first felt a solid sense of what that meant. That meaning has since been confirmed by many a warm conversation and by the solid vote of the Spawn himself: "Welcome, Psaunty Andrea!" he crows when I visit. (I'm sure he'll pronounce it right eventually.)

Part 2: The Spawnlet

Torsten

The four of us — me, Marcie, Erin, and Eli — were eating at my favourite Indian restaurant in Montreal in early 2007 when I asked Erin and Marcie if they were going to stop with Eli or if they wanted more children. Marcie said that they were thinking about it, and asked if I was interested. I felt very honoured, but I had to ask if they didn't want someone else to donate, so that they could have a different genetic mix.

"Who said I would carry the baby next time?" asked Marcie, and that stopped me dead. For some reason, I had never thought of any other possibility, perhaps because it was so obvious with Eli that Marcie would be the biological mother. Erin had repeatedly said that she had no interest in carrying a baby herself, but I guess things change when you see someone go through pregnancy as seemingly effortlessly as Marcie did, and when you have such a wonderful Spawn in your life. On my part, the answer was yes.

Marcie and Erin

A few years had passed, and Erin realized that having a baby was something she wanted to try after all. Eli was the only kid at too many functions. As Marcie reflected on the value of generational solidarity she had felt growing up with her own brother, we realized that there needed to be another kid. They would need each other to commiserate with as teenagers. And now that she is finally an actual paid (resident) physician, in Kingston, Ontario, Erin is the one who can score maternity leave.

Torsten

It struck me later to ask if Erin would be interested in perhaps not going the turkey-baster route, but instead going about the process in a way that was more ... old-fashioned. Or terribly cutting-edge, depending on the context. I'd always found her attractive, and thought and hoped (thanks to some hints about her sexual past) that she might be interested as well.

So the next time they were over at my place, as Marcie was

off putting a sleeping Eli in the car, I asked Erin about it. She froze for a second — at last, I'd surprised them rather than the other way around! — and said that she'd have to talk to Marcie. She seemed fairly neutral but didn't say no, so I guessed that she was interested, and it was now a matter of working out whether it was a good idea.

On my part I simply waited to see what the verdict was, as the intense conversation and negotiation took place on their part. When it looked like it was actually going to happen, I suddenly got very nervous. What if we weren't compatible, and it was a horrible experience? What if it did in fact ruin our relationship? What if I ended up being a clumsy, stupid guy in bed? There was more riding on this than just another spawn, and the weight of that quickly made itself felt.

Erin

Although Marcie and I have never been explicitly monogamous, neither of us had been in a significant romantic or sexual relationship outside our own in the nine years we had been together. Our community of family and friends had always been heavily polyamorous, but we had never made nurturing multiple relationships a priority. So when Torsten asked me if I wanted to try getting pregnant "naturally," I realized that things were about to get more complicated.

Amusingly, there was very little "natural" about explicitly fucking for babies. We eventually gave up the stressful project of getting pregnant in bed and moved to the comparatively less pressured environment of the fertility clinic. My sexual relationship with Torsten has continued past its baby-making beginnings, and we are still juggling time together and time with children in otherwise full schedules.

Torsten

In the end, logistics ended up being the worst of it. All that worrying about things at the higher levels of relationships devolved into the drudgery of finding insemination timing that worked for everyone. We were both nervous wrecks the first time. By the time the hemming and hawing was over, the sex felt less like sex than like a goal-oriented, time-limited activity. The nervousness never really left; every time we got together, the artificiality of the forced timing — along with the overall context and the effort to make time on short notice when the ovaries demanded it — overwhelmed the actual activity, try as we did to get beyond all of it.

Erin and I didn't talk about what was going on emotionally nearly as much as we had talked about anything during the process leading up to Eli. Maybe we felt like old hands at baby-making after such a wonderful success as Eli, or maybe all the energy that went into working out the scheduling and the frustration (as weeks went by and pregnancy remained depressingly remote) distracted us. In any case, emotions — not surprisingly — snuck in on their own as we raced against the clock.

After all that work it was a trip to the fertility clinic for a round of artificial insemination that finally did the trick. Before being inserted directly into Erin's uterus, my sperm were washed and, again, looked at on TV. Maybe we should have just tried putting them on camera for the first attempt instead of as a last resort. Erin became pregnant with the Spawnlet in early 2008.

Marcie and Erin

Turning noble thinking into flesh required time, planning, and sperm again. But this time there was already a spuncle in our family. Not just a "friendly captain of a spermatozoal swim team," but Torsten, who occupied this role with few models, and played it in a way that seemed to move well within the rhythms of our family. Giving the children a genetic link was a nice bonus, but giving them a happily functioning queer family was foremost in our minds. Our family has grown and morphed as many do, but the connections are less bound to bloodlines and sealed paper. Friends of friends become intricately woven, often by taking emotional risks, by making commitments, and by just being there — especially with the kids.

One such friend was Helen. We first met her through Maïda — the same Maïda who introduced us to Torsten through Jake —

when we were still just musing about potential baby-making. Over the course of the years that followed, our bond grew deeper ever so gradually, among other things thanks to our shared experience as queer women working in kids' camps and to Helen's delicious baking. We all have a hard time pinpointing when, exactly, she became family instead of simply our fun redhead friend, but as Eli grew older and the Spawnlet's creation progressed, she took on an ever-greater role as a supportive presence. When we moved to Kingston, her own blood-family connections there led to regular visits with us; soon enough she was taking turns with Jake and Dave hosting bi-monthly family dinners for whoever happened to be in Toronto, too.

Andrea

In June of 2007, when I was visiting Toronto to enjoy Pride celebrations, I met a wonderful trans boi named Mitch, and everything about us just made sense. By August, we were trolling Craigslist for an apartment. Somewhere in the middle of all this, I was introduced to Lindsay, and sparks flew; we became involved that same fall, and I moved to Toronto in January. By March 2008, Mitch and Linz also became lovers, so somehow I've found myself one very lucky woman in a triad with two bois. It didn't take long before they were each swept into the family as well — Linz and Jake bonded over shared chemistry-geekiness, Helen and Mitch over a love of good cooking, and all of us over pots of lentil stew whenever we're all miraculously in town at once.

Jake

It seems to me that families grow spontaneously around children. I never intended for Erin and Marcie to be such important parts of me, or for Andrea and her lovers to be family. I certainly never intended to be eyeing the "Someone who loves me very much goes to U of T" socks at school with such intent. We draw lines between "family" and "friend," based on blood or marriage, and as a result can consider ourselves closer to people we see every few years than to people we see once a week. But now people I barely knew well enough to call friends, people I still see only a few times a year — like Eli's back-up guardians and uncles, Bear and J — are without question part of my family. With Eli at the centre, those connections just appeared, and now I can't imagine life without them.

Andrea

Erin had asked me if I'd be willing to attend the Spawnlet's birth, which was expected in early December 2008. She felt that, as a sadomasochist, I could put my transferable skills to use in helping her manage the pain of childbirth. (Erin is nothing if not logical.) I agreed, though not before admitting it might be strange to gather with her, Marcie, and Torsten in such an emotionally charged situation. For all that Torsten and I are on good terms, we've never entirely resolved the sadness of our breakup, and I didn't want that spilling into the supportive atmosphere we wanted to create for Erin. But, we all agreed, we were grown-ups, and we'd figure it out.

In the late afternoon of November 5, 2008, I got a call from Marcie. Her voice was tense as she told me that Erin, at eight months' pregnant, had begun to hemorrhage that afternoon while doing her rounds at a medical clinic. She'd been rushed to hospital, and the baby had been delivered by emergency C-section. I found out later they'd both come perilously close to dying. Within a couple of hours, Mitch and Linz and I had rented a car, and we'd called Helen, Jake, and Dave to keep them apprised of the situation. Torsten was already on a bus from Montreal. We packed our bags, picked up Helen, and hit the highway, zooming into Kingston in the wee hours of the morning. The last thing Marcie said to me before we left was, "It would be great if you guys could start thinking about baby names."

And so the family converged. Thus begun several days of family care shift work: the bois on kitchen duty, Helen and Mitch alternating on Spawn care, Torsten spending his days at Erin's side, and Marcie sleeping on the floor most nights next to Erin's bed in the postpartum unit, while I tried to keep things flowing smoothly and support Marcie in all the craziness. Erin had lost a lot of blood and was very weak; we made sure she was never alone, and always well-fed, during visiting hours. Helen told me later of a moment in which Erin said groggily but with a grin, "This is my family. My wife, my lover, his ex, and her bois, and Helen, who has red hair."

The first time I laid eyes on the Spawnlet, she was encased in an incubator, a tiny, bright pink creature covered in tape and tubes. Although she was jaundiced and underweight, somehow, she didn't seem the least bit fragile. Her name — chosen by Marcie and Erin from our two-page list (with Jake's request that her first initial be *M*) and presented to the whole family as we gathered around Erin's bed — is Miriam Grey Gibson Sandilands. As soon as she came out of the NICU, she spent all her waking hours being passed from one family member to another, even to Bear and J, who made a detour through Kingston on their way back from one of Bear's speaking engagements. I snapped a picture of Bear holding her, his beefy hands dwarfing her tiny body as he cradled her with a tenderness I think all of us felt. We were all simply in awe of this miniature person whose emergence into the breathing world had brought us all together with such unquestioned urgency.

And it was okay. Erin is alight — drugs took care of the pain much more expediently than I could have, transferable skills or no, and she now sports an elegant, razor-thin scar across her abdomen. The weirdness between me and Torsten was minimal. Linz and the Spawn both got to hold a baby for the first time. Everyone got along.

Our time in the hospital did show us how people translate everything they see into the heterosexual nuclear-family template, such as when two people stopped Mitch and Helen as they were walking down the hall, holding the Spawnlet: "Oooh, heading home with your new baby? Congratulations!" None of us play our parts in this family out of a desire to be radical, but it's moments like that one that show us all just how unusual this family is, and how hard it is to describe the whole thing without sitting someone down and telling them a story. Fortunately, we've now managed to do exactly that — or at least, we've got the first couple of chapters down. The rest is playing out every moment of every day as two fantastic queerspawn kids grow, and as their family grows too.

Marcie and Erin

Like lots of families, we are a wildly imperfect creative process. Creativity is messy. So are sex, pregnancy, and birth. Creating — like pregnancy and childbirth — is also difficult, and occasionally exhausting. Navigating degrees of "outness" about being pregnant, about being polyamorous, and about being queer in a new and small city has kept us up late in conversations. In weary moments it seems as though emulating a family model that works for other people would be simpler, and give us time to just get the dishes done, dammit. But the rest of the time we are fantastically proud and thrilled to be a part of this multi-generational, polyamorous, and queer kinship project that (so far) seems to be working for the people involved.

Torsten

In the end, it's not just a tight nucleus of those who are in the byline of this story who make up this family. Rather, it's a sprawling, loving, organic web-like thing that continues to grow over time without strictly defined limits, and in our nuclear-family-obsessed society that's in some ways as radical as anything else that each of us, individually, might do or be.

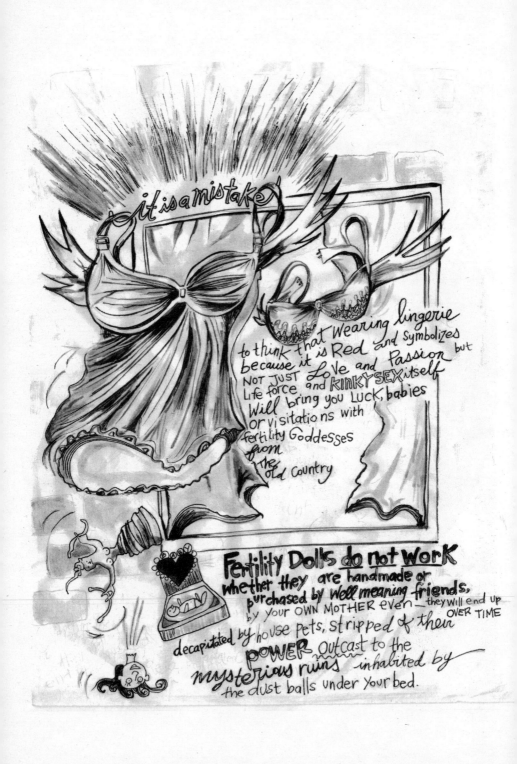

it is a mistake

to think that wearing lingerie
because it is Red and symbolizes
NOT JUST Love and Passion but
Life force and KINKY SEX itself
Will bring you LUCK, babies
or visitations with
fertility Goddesses
from
the old Country

Fertility Dolls do not WORK
whether they are handmade or
purchased by well meaning friends,
by your OWN MOTHER even — they will end up OVER TIME
decapitated by house pets, stripped of their
POWER outcast to the
mysterious ruins inhabited by
the dust balls under your bed.

Two Kids on their side, and one on ours needed to be put to bed before I could expect anyone to oblige my request for sperm. Most of our fertilization attempts were at night. Rebecca drove to Zio and Catherine's house, over and over through winter storms and heat waves, like a maniac with a jar of sperm in her cleavage.

I would make a Giant Effort to get Kealy to sleep before → she got home - so that we could have what I liked to think of as quality insemination time together

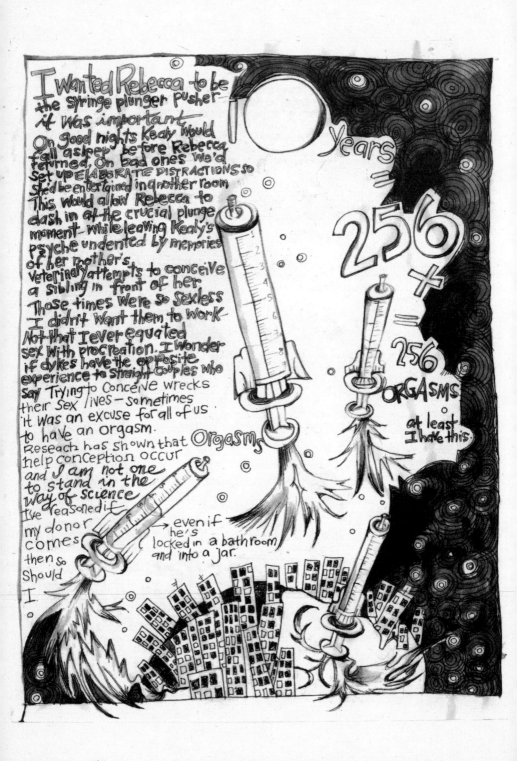

I wanted Rebecca to be the syringe plunger pusher - it was important. On good nights Kealy would fall asleep before Rebecca returned. On bad ones we'd set up ELABORATE DISTRACTIONS so she'd be entertained in another room. This would allow Rebecca to dash in at the crucial plunge moment while leaving Kealy's psyche undented by memories of her mother's veterinary attempts to conceive a sibling in front of her. Those times were so sexless I didn't want them to work. Not that I ever equated sex with procreation. I wonder if dykes have the opposite experience to straight couples who say trying to conceive wrecks their sex lives — sometimes it was an excuse for all of us to have an orgasm. Research has shown that orgasms help conception occur and I am not one to stand in the way of science. I've reasoned if my donor comes then so should I.

→ even if he's locked in a bathroom and into a jar.

10 years =

256 + = 256 ORGASMS

at least I have this.

Love is accidental. It just happens, like pregnancies. As we all went along love came too. Maybe it's in the gesture of passing body fluids in jars to each other. years of protecting something microscopic and imbued with possibility that needs to be kept warm. Maybe the very idea of this child created an invisible web between our familiies. Since they only existed in our minds, we all hoped for them making all four of us their parents of a kind. This is the part of the story of us all that has even less of a name then something not named at all. We are held together by grief for someone who didn't make it here. We each dug a space in ourselves to make room for them —offered ourselves, our bodies as bridges, but sometimes things don't turn out the way you think. Bread that took all day to make burns, the cookies were made with salt instead of sugar, the cake never rises. All they had to do was get here — make it from the heat of our bodies, the tangle of our hope and love to the noise and mess that was waiting for them here.

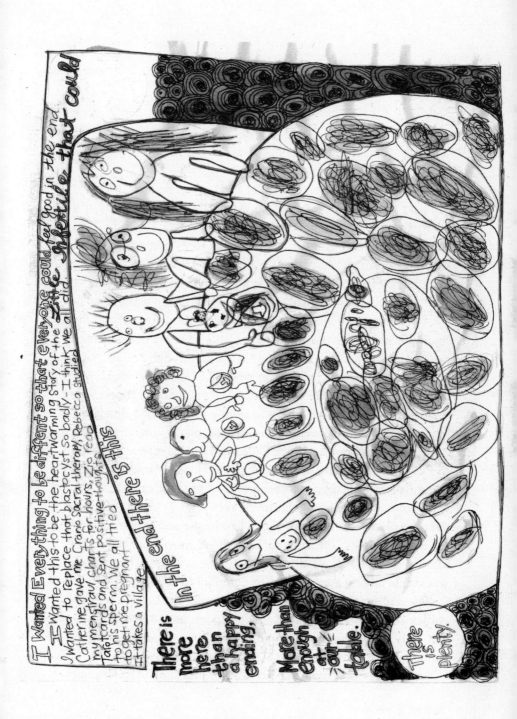

I Wanted Everything to be different so that everyone could feel good in the end

I wanted this to be the heartwarming story of the little infertile that could

I wanted to replace that blastocyst so badly- I think we all did. Catherine gave me Cranio Sacral therapy, Rebecca studied my menstraul charts for hours, Zia read Tarot cards and sent positive thoughts to his sperm. We all tried to get me pregnant

It takes a village.

In the end there is this

There is more here than a happy ending,

More than enough at our table.

There is plenty.

Spermbro

BY SUSAN COLE

When Molly plops herself down at the kitchen counter, I look at her with amazement. I always do. My partner, Leslie, and I still can't get over the fact that we created this creature with Leslie's egg, a syringe, and the most beautiful gift a guy could give: a teaspoon of sperm.

I ask Molly how she feels about her sperm donor.

"Well," she says with a frown. "I used to hate it when I had to fill out forms at school. I never knew what to do about the 'mother's name, father's name' part. That's what I remember about primary school. And when we were going through the adoption process, I had to go to that lawyer who asked me a bunch of really annoying questions. 'Are you aware that if your mother adopts you, you will no longer have access to your sperm donor's finances?' And on and on, as if I were losing, not gaining, something."

She has his brow — or the Cole brow, as it's referred to, with the low hairline — and when I lean over to kiss her head the smell is familiar: it's the unmistakable aroma of my brother's skin.

Today, you may see ads for "Dykes with Tykes" groups all over the place. But 22 years ago, when Leslie and I were looking for a sperm donor, the lesbian motherhood movement was in its infancy, so to speak. That meant that there was almost zero consciousness among men about their potential to help out their dyke friends and family by donating to the cause. And, since fertility clinics and sperm banks were dealing sperm at $10,000 a pop — and only to heterosexual couples, not even to single straight women — we had a tough time getting our hands on any.

As it was, our friends wanted to be helpful and did make some offers, but they just weren't the kinds of offers we were looking for. When we asked one of Leslie's close pals about it, he got really excited and started to talk about being at the birth. I felt a sudden rush of nausea. Another said he was interested, but his wife was having a hard time with the concept.

I lived with some deep-seated fears that began when the sperm search started and continued throughout Leslie's pregnancy and during Molly's younger years: who was I going to be in this relationship? If I wasn't the birth mother, would I have any connection to my child?

There were lots of other reasons for me to me to feel insecure. Leslie was trained as a skilled childcare worker, and I knew nothing about child-rearing. Leslie had always wanted a child whereas, ever since I'd come out in my early twenties, I had assumed I'd never raise a family. She was determined to be a mother. When she informed me that, if I wasn't interested, she'd be having a child anyway, it was a shock. We were very much in love, but it sounded as if she'd have given up our relationship if I hadn't been willing to have a child with her.

When we first dreamed up the idea of asking my brother Peter, it seemed like an inspired idea. Given my worries, the idea of having my brother on board was appealing. Apart from giving me a blood connection to our child, I was sure that having Peter as the sperm donor would ease the conversation with my parents about our decision to have children. It would be hard for them to discriminate against a grandchild with their genes.

My relationship with Peter was always good — we had even been close friends when I was in my twenties. He's a doctor with radical politics, and we'd done some decent political work together, including collaborating with other health activists to organize a conference on contraception.

The first time we approached Peter, he couldn't wrap his head around it. He said something about his fear that he'd feel too responsible. Feeling misunderstood and — given the sperm clinic's rejection — a little bit paranoid, we took his initial response as an indication that he'd want more control than we were prepared to give.

Months later, he changed his mind and agreed. I think the fact that his second marriage had dissolved had something to do with it, but, to give him some credit, he could also see that our desire was real and his personal sense of justice made him sympathetic to the fact that other men's reluctance and the medical system's discriminatory practices were getting in the way of that desire being met.

It took Leslie three cycles to get pregnant. Peter would come to the house with his five-year-old daughter, our niece, whom we'd take for a quick walk around our Kensington Market neighbourhood, returning in time to get the goods.

Leslie miscarried during her second trimester, which was devastating. I admit I did have a quick flash, not of relief, exactly, but a sensation of having avoided a life change I wasn't ready for. When Leslie birthed the fetus — at home, two weeks after she found out that it was no longer alive — I looked closely at it. Tiny, with just one leg, this baby boy was definitely not meant to come into the world. And I believe that at the time, I too, wasn't ready for motherhood. In a way, though traumatic, the miscarriage was a part of the preparation I needed to be a mother.

My brother was amazing — following the miscarriage he simply stepped right back in, ready to try again as soon as Leslie had had three periods. Leslie got pregnant with Molly just as my brother was falling in love with Ila, his current wife. This was an extremely important development: whenever I'm asked by lesbians for advice regarding a known donor who's not signing on as a co-parent, I stress this point: Find someone who's not emotionally needy and who has his own very busy life to live.

Giving life is a powerful thing. I'd like to think I'd be the first to say, "Back off, buddy," to an over-involved sperm donor, but I actually sympathize with men who get attached to what comes of their donation and who have trouble keeping their distance once the wondrous creature appears before them. We were very fortunate that, by the time Molly arrived in the world, Peter had a ton on his plate and was way too busy planning his own wedding and blending families to be worrying too much about us.

Leslie and I never made a clear decision about when and how we would tell Molly who her sperm donor actually was, though we did establish a few ground rules. We would wait until she asked, and when we told her about her origins, we would make sure my brother informed his own daughter, Sascha, about his special gift to us. But it took a while before we actually engaged in the conversation

"Why does Charlie at daycare say it's impossible for me not to have a father?" Molly asked one day. The answer was simple enough. Charlie's single mother was eager to convince her three-year-old son that, while his father may have been absent, he did exist (and of course loved him very much). But Leslie and I decided to make Molly's question our entrée into discussing the topic of her sperm donor.

We began by telling her that you need sperm from a man and an egg from a woman to make a baby. Leslie had previously attempted to explain these facts to Molly, only to get totally caught up in the penis inside the vagina thing, forcing me to intervene and say, "Enough of that — let's just stick to the sperm and the egg part."

Ever since we began reading to Molly, we'd put Lesléa Newman's *Heather Has Two Mommies* on the reading list. It tells the story of two lesbians who want to have a baby. Their process involves going to their doctor, who assists them in getting the sperm from an anonymous donor, whereupon the pregnancy happens, Heather's born, and they all live happily ever after. We began reading this book with the idea that we'd use it as a vehicle to tell Molly who her sperm donor was. Our theory was that, once we got to the sperm part of the story, Molly would ask us where our sperm came from. But that never happened. We'd get to the part about the sperm and wait for the shoe to drop. It never did. It was an important lesson in parenting: never expect your kid to bring up the subject you want to talk about.

One evening, the topic came up — I don't recall how (even recently, the three of us couldn't agree on the real story) — and Leslie finally asked outright, "Molly, have you ever wondered where we got the sperm to create you?"

"I know where you got it," she said. "You went to a special doctor, asked for the sperm, and the doctor got it for you from somebody you didn't know." Molly had heard that story about Heather and her two mommies, and she was sticking to it. We finally asked her outright if she wanted the information. When we said it was her uncle, she looked surprised.

"Someone I know," she said with a tone of wonder.

There it was: the moment I had dreaded. I think a lot of non-birth mothers relate. Where do we fit? How easily can we be supplanted? I was the one who dealt with the first poop of meconium — that slimy green stuff that comes out just after a baby is born — because Leslie found it too hard to handle. I learned from Day Two of Molly's life that my relationship with her could be like nobody else's. She knew I was on the A-Team. She could smell me, I know it. I wasn't as delicious as Leslie — I mean, I didn't have that gorgeous milk leaking out of my breasts — but I was there for her all the time, and she knew that. Still I had those fears. How powerful is that body connection, and what does it mean when we don't have it?

I still harbour vestiges of that panic. I can tell whenever the subject of adult adopted children seeking their birth mothers comes up. All right, I'll support their right to search, but I've never totally grasped why it's so important — except for medically related reasons — to find out anything about whoever gave birth to them. My irrational panic — really, why shouldn't adopted kids learn their pre-birth histories? — is all about my fear that these children feel like they have been missing something. As a non-birth mother, I am fundamentally frightened by the thought.

Despite not having a dad at home, our daughter never felt like anything was missing, even when Father's Day rolled around. She'd always make her school Father's Day project for my father, her Zaidie. And when Leslie asked Molly one day whether she ever wished she had a father, she said, without hesitation, "No, but I wish I knew more kids who had two mothers."

Astonishingly, once Molly got wind of who her sperm donor

was, absolutely nothing changed about her relationship with Peter. She didn't suddenly harbour fantasies of an increased connection. She never felt any weirdness in his presence. There was no sudden drama.

But just because Molly didn't necessarily want to open up a new and special relationship with my brother doesn't mean she didn't consider ways of taking advantage of this new tidbit of information. She's always been an expert at argument and logic. When she was still five and we were preparing for the holiday season, she argued that we should get a Christmas tree for the household. We celebrate Hanukkah and had never had a tree in the house. Why, we wondered, was this five year old, who always loved Hannukah, suddenly interested in a Christmas tree?

"My sperm's wife is Christian," she answered.

Twenty years later, I still experience the odd pang of fear. Even after adopting Molly five years ago, an experience that made me finally understand why so many gays were running to the altar — there's nothing like hearing a judge order something that signifies such a profound shift in the system — I wonder: Am I the real thing?

So it's something of a revelation to hear Molly talk about how she feels about having her uncle as her sperm donor.

"You mean to say," I ask her, "that discovering your biological origins didn't make you feel any closer to Peter?"

"Well, no, actually," she replies. "It made me feel closer to you."

The Miracle

BY BOB SMITH

My partner, Michael, and I had just climbed into bed and pulled up the comforter. We'd driven three hours northeast of Toronto and were staying in Elvira and Chloë's cottage, which they've named "Treehab" — a joke that I not only love, but also wish I'd thought of myself. It was the end of August, and the night was chilly. Summers in the north remind you, even on the hottest days, that the sun is a fire in the sky — when it goes out, the room grows cold. Before turning off the light, we overheard two-year-old Madeline having a conversation in the bedroom next to ours.

"Are Bob and Michael boys?"

Her sweet babyish voice made it sound as if she was inquiring about the gender of the Easter Bunny.

"Yes, honey," Elvira replied. "They're boys."

Michael and I chuckled quietly.

"I'm glad she cleared that up," Michael whispered.

"Maybe Maddie's confused because we're not as butch as some of their lesbian friends."

"Speak for yourself."

We were visiting Madeline and her parents for the weekend. Michael and I had flown from New York to Buffalo to see my mother and then headed north. Madeline had instantly taken to Michael, grabbing him by the hand. "Michael! Hurry! Come inside my house!" He obeyed promptly, entering the area near the sofa where her toy stove stood. "Bob! You too!" Madeline was at the delightful age where she spoke exactly like a children's book: short, declarative sentences that ended in exclamation marks. It's probably the only time in our lives when our conversation naturally emulates literature.

Four years earlier, Elvira and Chloë had asked me to be their sperm donor. I was surprised and flattered when they requested half of my chromosomes, and it made me realize why so many straight men are insufferably cocksure. A big part of the appeal of heterosexuality is that every act of sexual intercourse holds out the possibility of — reproduction — the condom could break, the diaphragm could leak, or the pill could be a placebo. Therefore, having sex with a woman is a pat on the back of every man's penis. Even for men whose DNA should be thought of as an abbreviation for "Do Not Approach."

Elvira had discussed having a baby with me a few years before she met Chloë.

"I want to do it the natural way," she said. "I think we'll only need to do it once." Then the comedian in her added, "Believe me, we'll only *want* to do it once." We both laughed. Elvira and I have been friends for many years. We first met when we performed stand-up together in Toronto, but became close when we lived together for two weeks in Sydney. We were performing at a queer comedy festival, and the performers lived in a lavish residential hotel where each room had two bedroom suites. When we arrived in Australia, the festival's producer told Elvira and me, "I've put the boys with boys and girls with girls except for you two. Somehow I know you'll get along." She was right. We were predisposed to become friends because we each thought the other was funny; it's impossible for a funny comedian to become close friends with a comedian who isn't. It's like a vegan falling in love with a butcher.

Before Elvira brought up the subject, I'd never really thought about reproducing. At least that's what I'd always believed until recently. A year ago, I moved from Santa Fe to New York and, while going through some files, found the proposal for my second book of comic essays. It was written years before Elvira asked me to become her donor:

Essay 3. On Being A — Father — Our friends Judy and Sharon recently had a baby, and our friends Nanette and Tommy have had their second child, and so [my then-boyfriend] Tom and I have officially become Gay Uncles. (Sharon asked us to consider becoming the father while Judy brutally and hilariously sized up our genetic pluses and minuses.) I would love to write about the possibility of becoming a father because to my astonishment, I actually think I would make a good one.

I'd forgotten that I'd written this. Reading it reminded me how much I'd changed since I first came out in the early eighties. Back then I presumed that my being gay precluded having children. In fact, I thought of it as one of the advantages. My friends and I never talked about children unless a baby was crying on an airplane. Most of us were aspiring artists, and artists feel overwhelmed providing daycare for their inner children, let alone nurturing a real kid.

Back then, I had one gay friend who had a daughter. Gary was in his early forties — most of us were in our twenties — and he had once been married to a woman. Gary's example of fatherhood seemed to be an aberration from the gay norm. The Reagan era was a time when American gay men and lesbians realized our government and much of the culture didn't care whether we died of AIDS. Their enmity actually did gay people a favour because when people are rooting for your death, they immediately lose any influence over telling you how to live. There was no direct connection between the homophobic Reagan administration and the deeply personal decision to have children, but it is interesting that many gay and lesbian families were started almost in defiance of open political discrimination.

In the mid-nineties, Sharon and Judy, two of my closest friends, decided to start a family. It was decided that Sharon would have their first child and Judy their second. I naively assumed that lesbians could afford to be ruthlessly discriminating when picking a sperm donor. I didn't know then how difficult in can be to find a donor and imagined if all women were as selective as lesbians we'd have evolved into a race of Gods by now. Like most of us, my family has genetic pluses and minuses. My Dad died of alcoholism, and my mother and sister have both suffered from depression, which makes me think of my DNA as a make-it-a-double helix. On the plus side, I've never been prone to depression, have tried to keep my booze and pot intake recreational instead of vocational, and I'm smart, funny, and when I look back at photos of myself in my late twenties, I find it hard to believe I never thought I was handsome. This may sound conceited, but there is one thing I do know: If you can't admit your virtues after forty, you won't make it to fifty. Our biggest drawback as donors for Judy and Sharon was that Tom and I were goys; they wanted a Jewish donor and didn't buy my argument that every successful stand-up comedian should be considered part-Jewish. There were no hard feelings on my part when Sharon chose an anonymous Jewish donor.

It took Sharon almost a year to get pregnant. Sometimes, after she went to the doctor to get inseminated, I'd suggest the two of us should lie in bed and smoke cigarettes in order to increase the chances of her getting knocked up. When Sharon eventually gave birth to Henry, it was a joyous event for everyone. I became his "Uncle Bob," and the two of us developed a rapport almost immediately. I'm not exactly sure what it is that he liked about me, although I always answered his questions without talking down to him. This wasn't a conscious strategy to win Henry's affection but more a response to my own childhood resentment of being treated as, well, a child and my fond memories of the times when I'd been treated like an adult. In the second grade, my teacher, Miss Rockwood, realized my interest in dinosaurs wouldn't be satisfied by children's books and, to my gratification, urged me to read a young adult book about Roy Chapman Andrews's discovery of dinosaur eggs in the Gobi desert. When I was in the fifth grade, I loved that my grandmother would always bring me last week's copy of *Newsweek* because I followed current affairs — cheering on the Czechs when the Russians invaded in 1968.

When Henry was very young, we took him to Disneyland and he insisted on sitting next to me on all the rides. The night before, as we left a restaurant, Sharon said, "Henry, you need to put on your jacket." He twisted up his face into a small fist of protest. Sharon shot me a conspiratorial look. "Uncle Bob is wearing his jacket," she said. Henry looked up at me and, without another word, put on his jacket. Sharon leaned over to me, "Isn't it nice that someone idolizes you?" "Nice" hardly did justice to the elation I felt.

It was entirely gratifying because children's affection is straightforward. There's no underlying agenda of sucking up to you because you can advance a child's career selling lemonade or boost their reputation by attending their next show-and-tell presentation. Henry liked me because he liked me. And I liked him. He was curious about everything and cracked jokes almost from the time he began talking. Henry has always been able to talk about his feelings, which made me feel I could also talk about mine. When I took Henry to the Museum of Natural History, I could say, "Look, we all want to have fun today and so I don't want any crying." After Henry's brother Ben was born, when I'd take them to the playground, I'd say the same thing and add, "No fighting." And for the most part there wasn't any crying or fighting.

My relationship with Henry profoundly changed how I thought about children. The first time I babysat for him, I brought the *New York Times*, assuming that I'd read the paper while he played a game or watched television. No. Henry insisted that I play with him for the entire time — for five hours. When Judy returned from her television taping, I admitted. "I don't know if I could do this full-time."

"Now you know why I'm exhausted all the time," Judy said.

"How did our mothers do it?" My mother had four children, and Judy's had three.

"With Librium," Judy said. "I'd be drinking vodka gimlets for breakfast if I had four kids."

After spending the morning with Henry, I was aware that I probably wouldn't like being a full-time parent.

A couple of years after Elvira met Chloë, the two of them asked me to be their sperm donor. When I said yes, they were ready to begin baby-making ASAP, which suddenly gave me qualms. I barely knew Chloë; I'd liked her immediately, but then every gay man has a history of meeting guys he likes immediately and despises later. It was awkward to admit that I needed more time; I wanted to get to know Chloë better and feel as close to her as I did to Elvira. I also wanted to be clear about exactly what our roles would be. Soon after, Chloë and Elvira visited me in Los Angeles, where we talked about everything, and then I visited them in Toronto. During several months of discussions we agreed they would be the parents and I would be the funcle; the baby would know I was her biological father but I would be the baby's Bob. We discussed what would happen if the two of them split up, and they assured me that I would always be a part of the baby's life. My reasoning was that since I trusted Elvira and Chloë to raise our baby, I could trust that they weren't going to screw me. Friends counselled me to get a legal contract, but I didn't want to do that. For me, this was an emotional commitment among all of us — a commitment that would last our lifetimes. While we weren't going to live together as a family, we were choosing to become Family.

When I finally said, "Yes. Let's do it," I had no doubt that it was the right decision; I looked forward to spending time with Elvira and Chloë for the rest of my life, and the decision felt comparable to the other major decisions I had made: deciding in 1983 that I had to move to New York or deciding in the late eighties that I had to try to become a stand-up comedian. I made those decisions knowing that something could go wrong, and they might end disastrously, but I also knew that I'd deeply regret not trying them.

Before we tried to have a baby, I needed to be tested for sexually transmitted diseases and also needed to have a sperm count done. In California, you can't have a lab do a sperm count without a doctor's prescription, and I was warned not to mention I was gay because many labs refuse to test gay men. Fortunately, a friend of mine, Jason, had just graduated from medical school. When I told him my problem, he wrote me a prescription. Jason was gay and actually got a kick out of screwing the homophobic medical system. When I went for my sperm test, the jerk-off room had several issues of *Hustler* magazine, which made me think less of some of the donors and made me wish I'd brought a sample of gay porn to leave as reading material. My test results were good; it turned out my boys could swim, and I had no STDs. We were ready to go.

My first donation took place at my house in Los Angeles. No doctor was involved — the gals were do-it-yourselfing their baby. It felt like we were doing a science fair project. I went into my bedroom and masturbated into a disposable clear plastic cup, part of me wondering if the kid would come out looking like the guy I fantasized about. After a short while, I emerged, hot cup of Joe or Josephine in hand. Elvira came out of their room, grabbed the cup, thanked me and returned to their room and closed the door. It was definitely awkward for all of us, but none of us commented on it until weeks later in Toronto when my jerking off into a cup several times a day had become as commonplace as doing the dishes. I realized that we might have become too comfortable on the day I brought my cup upstairs, and Chloë was on the telephone. When she saw me, she said to whomever she was speaking, "I'm sorry, I've got to go. Bob and I are inseminating this morning." I suggested her declaration would be the perfect way to fend off unwanted phone solicitations.

While we were trying to get pregnant, I told my mother that Elvira and Chloë had asked me to be their donor. I braced myself for a negative reaction, but my mother's response wasn't critical. She asked me how raising the child would work and if I'd thought carefully about all the ramifications. Her questions were thoughtful and practical. She'd met Elvira and Chloë and had immediately liked them. After I explained what my role would be — deadbeat donor — she gave her blessing: "All right." Then she said as an afterthought, "Children are wonderful, but you're opening yourself up to the possibility of great pain." She looked at me intently, making me think that she was referring to my sister's suicide. Her comment made me reflect on how courageous it is to have a child. Unconditional love also holds out the threat of unconditional pain. Her words weren't meant to shake my resolve; they were more of a comment on how much both my mother and I missed my sister.

A few weeks later, my mother called, and I told her I was packing for a flight to Toronto.

"For the miracle?" she asked, which made both of us laugh.

When Chloë and Elvira called to tell me we were pregnant, I experienced the thrilling elation that's always portrayed in television shows and movies and that I'd never experienced. It was a moment of rapturous joy. I was performing with my friends and colleagues in Key West in a show called Funny Gay Males. When I broke the news to them, Danny, one of the Males, responded, "Oh, Mrs. Smith, you're going to be a mother!"

Chloë was six months pregnant when she and Elvira were married in Toronto. As their best man, I was horribly tempted, as comedians often are, to introduce myself to their family and friends with a joke. "Hi, I'm Bob," I imagined myself saying. "I'm the best man who knocked up one of the brides."

When it got closer to the baby's due date, we discussed the actual birth. Chloë and Elvira wanted the birth to be an intimate event between the two of them and asked nicely if I would wait to visit the baby after he or she was born. Their request seemed reasonable to me; I didn't mind not being at the baby's birth because I hadn't been at the conception either.

They were convinced the baby was a boy while I had no doubt she was girl. I can't explain my certainty other than a gut feeling that after my sister's death, which had been devastating for me, that another woman would enter my life. My conviction wasn't based upon any belief in reincarnation; it was based upon a belief in symmetry: an important woman had left my life and the universe owed me one.

I wanted Chloë and Elvira to feel that the baby was theirs, although I did insist on being the first person they called after the baby was born.

Elvira called and left me a message on November 26, speaking in a low voice — she was in Chloë's hospital room, trying not to wake her — announcing the birth of Madeline. I've received several birth announcement calls, and the caller's voice is always suffused with unmistakable joy with a note of incredulity and relief.

Every sentence sounds like it's punctuated with a question mark. Listening to the message, I realized how relieved I was by the news. You avoid thinking of all the horrible things that could go wrong, but those fears can't be shaken until the baby makes an actual appearance. During her pregnancy, Chloë had pre-eclampsia, and her health was as much a concern for us as the baby's. I immediately called my mother.

"Oh, isn't that wonderful!" she said.

Meeting Madeline for the first time, I wondered if I'd feel some special connection with her and worried that maybe I wouldn't. We met when she was one month old. I'd already seen photographs of her and was relieved that she looked cute. (Other, less-partial observers told me they also thought she did.) Shortly after I arrived, Madeline fell asleep in my arms. While I lay on the couch for two hours she slept on my stomach and all the tender feelings of love I hoped would appear, did.

From the start Maddie has been wildly enthusiastic about being alive. Her first word was "Wow!" (I'm still not certain this wasn't part of an incomplete exclamation, "Wow! All three of you are queer?") Every time I see Maddie I observe new aspects of her — her love of drawing with watercolour markers, her excitement at holding a tiny frog in her palm, her telling me that she wants to paddle the canoe and then her discovery that it's much better to be a passenger as she hands me the oar. People are always asking me, "Does she resemble you?" Physically she doesn't. She has blue eyes and blond hair, but her love of frogs is mine and so, unfortunately, is her desire to have someone else paddle.

One of the unexpected bonuses of becoming a deadbeat donor is that it became a new source of material for my stand-up act. People always assume that comedians do everything for material, but — honestly — it didn't occur to me. But then I'd make a remark to a friend, like, "I love that there are gay parents now. Twenty years ago, did anyone ever think that one day bottles of poppers and lube would need childproof caps?" And, of course, then I said it onstage — and it's gotten a big laugh.

After Madeline was born, my mother wanted to send a gift for the baby. A dress and card were sent, followed a month later by Christmas presents and a card. Then a New Year's card and a Valentine, St. Patrick's Day and Easter cards — basically every holiday except for Arbor Day and Lincoln's birthday. It soon became apparent to all of us that while I wasn't going to be Madeline's Dad, my mother was going to be one of Madeline's grandmothers. This concerned me because I hadn't discussed it with Elvira and Chloë. It made sense because my mother had no other grandchildren. For almost 40 years, my mother has played pinochle with the same group of women, and she'd said enviously to me several times in the past, "All the girls in Card Club talk about their grandchildren. I'm sick of it." Chloë and Elvira quickly dispelled any concerns I had that my mother might be infringing upon them because they happily dubbed my mother "Grandma Sue." A trade imbalance of baby clothes from Buffalo soon followed.

My mother's unconditional love for Madeline gratified me. And her love was clearly unconditional because when we heard at her first birthday party that Maddie was using her tiny fingernails like a velociraptor, scratching kids at her daycare, my mother laughed approvingly. "She's a pistol!" Later when Maddie swatted me and cut my upper lip, my mother appeared to be delighted. "She won't take anything from anyone!" When I checked my gashed lip in a mirror, I realized I wasn't upset either. I loved that at the age of one Maddie already displayed the attitude of a tough biker chick wielding a switchblade: "Don't fuck with me or I'll cut you!" My response reminded me of my father's to my three-day suspension in the eighth grade for fighting. He seemed more pleased than upset when he heard the news.

Giving my mother Maddie has given me a leg up in my mom's esteem. And I'm also not above using Maddie to get my way with her. Before an election I always worry that my Republican brothers will sway my mother to vote for their repulsive candidates. Now, I use my trump card. I remind my mother that the Republicans are anti-gay. "You know, Mom. If Madeline lived here, the Republicans would be against her parents." And I'll add, "They're also anti-environmental. So Madeline will inherit a shitty planet." It thrills and amuses me when my mother responds, "Those bastards!"

I don't dwell on the hardships or dangers Madeline might face or the sorrow she might experience because I'm consumed with the slightly more comforting anxiety that I might be the one to hurt her. About a year after Madeline was born, I was diagnosed with a serious neurological disease; I'm doing well, but while I worry about my health, I also worry about Madeline. I'm afraid I'll die before she's old enough to know or even remember me, and I'm immodest enough to think that people who don't know me are missing out on something terrific.

There are so many things I want to share with Maddie: for example, how marvelous that she's Canadian because my father was born in Canada, and she comes from a long line — she's eighth- or ninth-generation Canadian. Her direct ancestor Nicholas Smith fought with Butler's Rangers during the American Revolution, something that I never learned until my mid-40s. I'd also like to tell Maddie about My List of Things That Won't Disappoint You. It's a list of wonderful things and experiences that I've kept for years because I think it's important to remember that many wonderful things have happened in my life. My list begins with redwood trees. I can guarantee that no one will ever see a redwood and say, "I don't see what's the big deal." Whales are also on the list. When you see a humpback whale breach, you'll never sigh, "That sucks." I'd also add seeing a comet with your naked eye. A field of almost fluorescent orange California poppies in bloom will never elicit a yawn. And New York City, Paris, and London will never ho-hum you. I want to tell her to visit Chaco Canyon in late August/early September when the purple asters have blossomed. And Maddie's already sampled one of the foods that makes everyone happy: maple syrup. ("Now I'm sure there are a few people who hate maple syrup," I'd warn her. "We call them kill-joys, and you should steer clear of them.") There's so much more: you should see the Acropolis at night, fall in love, and re-read your favourite book at 20 when you turn 40.

I also have a small store of wisdom that I'd like to impart to Maddie: my belief that it's okay to be skeptical but never to be cynical; my one litmus test for all religions: never believe in a God who's meaner than you are. (And I'm limiting the "you" in that sentence to Maddie and myself because you — the reader — could be a nasty nutjob.) My most important piece of advice would be to have fun, something Maddie already understands instinctively. Don't take anything too seriously; I want to tell Maddie about the first time I visited Walden Pond, a place I revere. But I still couldn't resist calling my friend John on my cellphone and leaving him a message because it was so wrong to have good reception there. I want to be around when Maddie can fully appreciate that irony.

On our last day at the cottage, the four grown-ups were sitting at the picnic table while Maddie covered the deck in bright coloured chalks. Suddenly a loon called out on the lake, a sound that is always called "haunting" —although that word has never seemed precise to me. The connotation of haunting is too sombre for such an exhilarating cry. Maddie kept drawing, which was fine because she'll have many opportunities to hear a loon, but Michael had never heard a loon before. Then the loon flew over our heads and cried again, something I'd never observed before. I'd add one more thing to my list of "Things that Won't Disappoint You": sharing something wonderful with the people you love.

Intimacy Constellation

BY ROSI GREENBERG

My mother said, "We were creating the role of 'donor,' really pioneering a social role. Someone who contributes to life and isn't in the role of raising the kid, but doesn't just disappear. It was a totally new thing at that time."

It was 1987, and my mom was beginning to craft a vocabulary to fit the life she planned to live. There's power in owning the language that describes your life, a sort of magic of normalcy for even the most alternative of families. I grew up with terms like "donor dad" to explain where the sperm came from to make me, "out-of-the-box" to explain my mom's sexuality, "parenting partner" to explain who was cooking dinner every Sunday. I didn't question where the terms came from; they were just always part of my "intimacy constellation."

In some ways, I was able to use words as my foot soldiers. I knew that not everyone had the sort of family that I did, but I had words for my family, and I could put them forth and explain the relationships on my own turf. Then, if the persona I was talking to didn't understand, it must have just been the words.

I'm 21 years old now, and I'm writing this piece as a student at an Ivy League university. I haven't always been so comfortable with the various parts of my broader family, or with sharing our vocabulary. But now, I hope that maybe my words can inspire the vocabularies of other families.

For a creative non-fiction assignment this year, I decided to tackle the strange relationship that is "donor dad," using mine, Avram, as my research subject. There have been times when I've connected to him only as those words — "donor dad" — and not really as a person, someone with whom I have a relationship. I often feel like I should know more about his life, since so many people do (he's a well-known rabbi), but I haven't read his books and don't feel connected to religion in his way. He doesn't usually tell me much about his life, because there are so many other sources that I can research by myself. I called him and asked him about how he saw me, and what "donor dad" meant to him.

He said, "There used to be a way to say that you were engendered by a donor and then it was supposed to be silent as to who was the donor. But it wasn't long — at the time you were a toddler — that your face gave away that you were a sister of Sophie and, oh, that you belonged to this *mishpakha,* this family. And it was whispered about but it didn't quite come out, I think, until your mom and I and Deborah we decided to let the word out ...."

My mother chose to be a single mom. She used to think that her ideal husband would be an airline pilot, because he would be away most of the time and she could get good deals on flights. At some point, she realized that she didn't have to get married at all, and she did it her own way, weaving together an incredible community in which to raise her children.

That's the three-sentence summary I usually give, with a laugh somewhere in there, to normalize it for others when I know it's heard as weird. What I usually don't say is that Deborah was married to Avram, and that my mom and Deborah were lovers.

My mother said, "It was [Deborah's] idea that I should ask Avram to be the donor father. She was completely happy for it, and I think she knew that one of the great things she had done in her life was to make you possible."

Sometimes I don't mention that part because it's private; other times I don't say it because it's too "not normal" to be heard respectfully.

When I was three my mother gave me hints and told me that I could guess who my donor dad was. She didn't tell me directly, she says, because she wanted it to come from me. "He has a long beard," she remembers saying, "We visit him sometimes and call him Big A."

"Avram!" she says I said, her three-year-old-me voice squealing as she performs the story.

When I was four, I decided I wanted to be a donor dad for Halloween. When my mother asked me what I would wear for a costume, I responded, "Well, I think I'll be, like, a big sperm." Interesting that the sperm was the most important part of "donor dad" for me then. My mother says she steered me in another direction, and I ended up being Abiyoyo the Giant.

A couple years later, a kid in Hebrew school didn't understand the concept of single mother.

"Where's your father?" he demanded of me over the two-forked family tree outline. Although I knew the Hebrew words for all the relatives, I also knew that my family was too "out of the box" for me to complete the assignment "properly," to get an A.

And I said, "I don't have one."

He persisted: "Everyone has a father."

"Where's your brother?" I asked.

"I don't have a brother, silly," he said.

And I said, "Well I don't have a father," and resolutely coloured the tree trunk brown.

When I was seven, Avram got married to Susan. I suppose I remember dancing on his feet at that wedding. I was wearing a pink dress — I think it was too big — and a white sweater that got lost that night. We had the picture on our fridge for years. I suppose I remember the picture, really, of me dancing on his feet, not the actual event.

Avram continues, "Since that time, watching both the way in which you combined inside of yourself your mom and me, was really remarkable. Both in your features but the, how would I say, the genotype that was the same as the females in our family. That was very strongly in your face, and that shows in that picture that you have with Sophie and you together. My heart is so full when I see that photo on the refrigerator."

A lot of our "donor dad" relationship seems to happen through pictures. Every time we see each other we snap a photo on whatever new digital gadget Avram's got.

Avram's student Adam became the donor dad for my brother Max in 1989 and my sister Lea in 1991.

Marcy, my mom's roommate and then lover when I was a baby, rocked me to sleep every night until I was two. Even after she moved out, she had the intimate role of carrying the sperm between Adam's room and my mother's room during Max's conception. A year later, Marcy and Adam were married and moved away, but not before participating in Lea's conception. They had a son, who is my seventeenth semi-sibling (he's the half-sibling of my half-siblings, so, technically, he's my quarter-sibling).

The next addition to our circle of loved ones was Rachel, whom my mom dated for many years. Rachel and her children brought the term "moose" into our family, as in "Hey moose, could you set the table?" or, "Come cuddle with me, moose." Rachel's children, Tali and Dani, and I used to call ourselves the "potato-scarf-mozzarella-parmesan-whatever-we-were-wearing-or-doing-or-eating-at-the-moment sisters," but now we've grown up, graduated to "potato-scarf-mozzarella-etc-etc-Palestine-activist-gender-nonspecific siblings" to accommodate changing political attitudes and shifting concepts of gender.

In 1996, my mom adopted Alex, my brother, from Guatemala, and we added the term "multiracial" to our definition of family.

Despite — or perhaps because of — parental break-ups, geographical moves, and children's growing up, the embrace of our intimacy constellation is flexible; relationships change but people remain in deep connection.

Lev became my mother's parenting partner, another new social role. Lev is gay, and my mom is "out of the box," so their relationship is emotional and intellectual, but not romantic. It took me a while to accept the new addition to the family: Lev was the photographer for my Bat Mitzvah, and many pictures of that twelve-year-old me include my middle finger.

But now, I embrace both the man and the vocabulary. A parenting partner is someone who participates in family in every aspect: dinners, decisions, rides, photos, and above all, love. Lev is my mom's parenting partner, my younger siblings' daddy, and my, well, my Lev. We don't actually have a word for his relationship to me, and it doesn't really matter.

Our family became complete when my mom and Lev adopted Lizzie from Guatemala in 2000. One day, when Lizzie was two, on a whim I conducted a linguistic experiment and told her that "Da" meant, "I love you." From then on, that's been our special thing: we touch noses and say "Da."

The family doesn't look the same from all angles. Last year I said something about having a single mom in front of seven-year-old Lizzie, who exclaimed, "Nuh uh! You have a mommy and a daddy!"

"No, *you* have a mommy and a daddy," I explained, "and you even have a birth mommy and daddy, but I have a mommy and a Lev and a donor dad. And we get to be sisters, and I think that's great."

This past year I traveled a lot in Palestine/Israel, where not many people understand the concept of "single mother" or "parenting partner" or "donor dad." "What does your father do?" taxi drivers would ask. "Oh, he's a history teacher," I'd invent, averaging out my rabbi donor dad and Lev, a Hebrew school teacher, into one, sort of amorphous, father-type-thing. In Arabic, I say my mother is a psychologist, my father is a history teacher, and I have four siblings. I let my listeners assume what they will about the marital status of my parents, the biological status of my siblings.

In high school, I went on a trip to Mexico with kids from a fancy suburban private school. During a long delay in the airport, I started telling my family history. They became more and more interested. I realized for the first time that my family was cool, a sort of social capital to be used to cultivate intrigue in anyone from fancy suburban kids to college admissions counsellors.

For a few years, the language around my family story became a performance, with pauses for effect, comic relief, gestures as Marcy marched between Adam's and my mother's bedrooms.

But some element of that performance felt like hiding behind e language, rather than truly expressing pride about my family. I took the interest my exoticism evoked as acceptance, rather than the voyeurism it may have been. I've become careful about my words, choosing the language I use to speak about my life, where and how I want to express it.

I asked Avram what he thought of telling this story. "I think you should do it in a lyrical way," he said. "In a lyrical way you can say something about how each time I saw you, from the time you were small, how my heart was happy. And you can feel it right now, can't you? So that's very much the thing. Before *Shabbes*, when I go to light the candles, and I check in my heart, you're always there. So, you know, these are very deep things. There's the business of how people can't really make sense of the word 'God'… that there is a heart connection to 'God,' it isn't only head, you know. The universe, the cosmos, is not blind to feeling you, that it knows you, that it's supporting you."

Every Friday night, we gather around my great-grandmother's table and light the Shabbat candles together. In the glow my mother chants, "We send *Shabbes* light to everyone who helped make this family, to Avram and Adam and Marta Eliza and Jose Lopez and Orbelina Del Carmen Rivera, and to Ashby and to Holly and Grandpa Ben and Sandy and Grandma Irene and to Lev and to Rosi and to Max and to Lea and to Alex and to Lizzie."

"What shines through is love," my mother said. "It's a good thing to be born out of love, and such intentionality."

Family… intentionality and a heart connection … the universe, the cosmos, is not blind to feeling you, that it knows you, that it's supporting you … an intimacy constellation.

How to Populate
the Earth with Your Progeny

BY HEATHER JOPLING

My name is Heather. I am not a lesbian. My husband David isn't gay. We are white, middle-class, heterosexuals and reside in a small Ontario town. We have one eight-year-old daughter, Rissa, who is healthy and happy. In 2003, in the privacy of our faux-Tudor suburban home laboratory, David provided teaspoons of precious sperm in a sterilized syringe for our lesbian friends Veronica and Carolyn. After four attempts, Veronica became pregnant and gave birth nine months later to a healthy baby boy — who, coincidentally, shares Rissa's birthday.

In 2004, again in our faux-Tudor suburban home laboratory, I became pregnant via the same syringe method (different syringe), using sperm provided by our gay friends Michael and Ernst, the fathers of the baby to be. In February of 2005, I gave birth to a baby girl in the presence of my husband, Michael and Ernst, a midwife, and a midwifery student.

Now, you may be asking yourself "Why?" Why would a relatively sane, straight, suburban, small-town couple decide to offer our DNA in the abstract and my womb in particular to two separate same-sex couples? For both of us the answer was simple: it was the right thing to do. We weren't trying to change the world; it really just seemed like the right thing to do. We had friends who wanted to have babies; we liked and respected these friends; they were unable to have babies on their own, so we helped them. Beginning of story.

The funny thing is, before knocking up this particular lesbian couple, David and I had already discussed the possibility of his providing sperm for another lesbian couple that we knew, one half of which was a childhood friend of his. We were new parents, and as new parents, you always wonder when your friends might have kids. You think to yourself, "They would make great parents. I wonder if they're going to try." When those friends happen to be lesbians you wonder *how* they might try to get pregnant. David thought, "Hey, maybe I could help them do that!" This initial thought was followed by more in-depth soul-searching. What would that mean for our own family? Would it ruin our friendship with these people if there were problems? What relationship, if any, would we have with the child? How much would we *want* to be involved with the child? How much would *they* want us to be involved with the child? Would this child have an emotional bond with us? What would our financial responsibilities be to this child? Could we watch them use a different parenting style than ours? We weighed the "what ifs," together and discovered we were both still comfortable with the idea and with the unknowns. So the next year, when we found out that our friends Veronica and Carolyn were trying to have a baby, it wasn't a difficult leap for us. We talked freely and openly with them about all of our expectations. Both families seemed to be on the same page.

There's another little fact that I should probably mention. Before even entering this realm, we had decided that we didn't want any more kids of our own. We were thrilled with our own daughter and had decided by the time she was three that our family was complete. So when the notion of sperm donation came up, we were looking at it as a favour for friends, not as another chance to parent a child.

When Veronica became pregnant, we drew up a "donor contract" with her and Carolyn that basically ensured that David would be neither emotionally nor financially responsible for the upbringing of the baby. Nor would he have any sort of parental role for the child. The only thing that David and I wanted to ensure was that we would be last in line for guardianship should anything happen to its parents. We would not be the child's godparents, or even the second choice for godparents, but rather, the last "family" before said child would go into the foster care system. David would give up his parental rights, and Carolyn would then adopt the child. And there the story could have ended, if it hadn't been for the annual *Chanumas* Party.

Chanumas is the amalgamation of Chanukah and Christmas. It is an event that Veronica and Carolyn, along with two of their friends, created — an annual event born long before Chrismukah came into vogue via the TV show *The O.C.* This particular *Chanumas* Party found Veronica four months pregnant and just about to share the news with all her friends. We had arrived early at the party, as had a mutual friend, Michael, his husband, Ernst, and their daughter, Klara, whom they had had via a surrogate. The kitchen was too small for many people to mingle, so Ernst and I were shooed away and sat in the living room.

I hit it off right away with Ernst. It was one of those instantaneous friendships. We chatted about parenting, loving our kids, peer pressure, how the "to breastfeed or not" issue doesn't get the same airplay with gay dads. Ernst said they were still hoping to find another surrogate — that he wanted as many kids as he could. "How many is that?" I asked. "Oh, at least five," he replied. "Well, more power to you," I said, thinking he was insane. But as I was listening to him, I found myself marveling at this man whose ideas of parenting seemed to mirror mine so completely. The glimmer of a thought began to tickle the back of my brain.

Later that evening, Michael and I stood beside Veronica as she announced that she was pregnant. As the guests erupted into spontaneous, supportive applause, Michael mouthed to Veronica, "Who's the father?" Putting her arm around me, Veronica replied, "It's David. They are a *very...* giving family. Heather even said that she might act as a surrogate for us if we hadn't managed on our own."

And that, officially, is when I heard the soft "click" of the light bulb that went on in my head. "*Really?*" Michael said, in a tone that suggested he saw a similar light.

"I think I might like to have a baby for Michael and Ernst," I told David on the drive home.

David looked at me in stupefied astonishment. "Are you nuts?"

"Probably."

"Heather, you could never give the baby up," he said.

"No ... I think I could. I really think that I could," I replied.

"Why ... why would you want to? I know that you didn't have a great pregnancy with Rissa — this wouldn't just be an excuse for a better pregnancy, would it?" (I'd had an unsatisfying birth experience with my own daughter, and had joked afterwards about being a surrogate so that I could have another shot at it and maybe get it right the second time around.)

I thought for a moment. "No. Not entirely. That might be a part of it, but really, that's not why I think that I could do this."

"Why would you do it, then?"

"David, they're such great parents. They want more kids. It would be so amazing to be able to help them have a baby. If I could be the person to give them this, then I should."

And then, even crazier, I actually did it. That's not to say that there weren't hiccups along the way. Michael and Ernst and I tentatively communicated via email for a bit, sussing out the situation and trying to figure out if we shared the same mindset. I had second thoughts; but not for the reasons that you would think. My second thoughts were because our local community theatre was doing a production of *Man of La Mancha*, and if I was pregnant I couldn't be in the show. I wouldn't have the opportunity to play Aldonza, the part I'd always wanted to play. I had second thoughts about having to pee on a fertility strip every morning and having to chart my ovulation.

I also had second thoughts about what would happen to my body after — not to mention during — the pregnancy. I had only just rid myself of the last pregnancy pounds from Rissa, and now here I was contemplating getting them back, and not even for *my* family. Frankly, pregnancy the first time around hadn't been that spectacular an experience. I'd become nauseated a week after conception, suffered Braxton Hicks contractions from week 28 on, and had blinding migraines. Every joint in my body swelled. Then, I had an emergency C-section two weeks past my due date.

In spite of all of this, I still decided to be a surrogate.

The first attempt to get pregnant did not go well. Michael was traveling past our town, and even though I wasn't technically ovulating, we thought we'd give it a try. Michael handed me the syringe and left me to my business. I inserted the syringe and deposited the sperm. I lay on my bed, feeling decidedly icky, a whole mess of (not my husband's) sperm inside me. All I could think was, "I have another man's spooge in me, and I think I'm getting a bladder infection." Which, of course, I did. We couldn't try the next month because I was on antibiotics.

The second try was more successful. I proceeded to have a wonderful pregnancy. I exercised every day, ate well, and didn't gain as much weight as I had with my own daughter. I was one of those fabled pregnant women who glowed. I had some nausea and the occasional migraine, but this time around I wasn't terrified to take Tylenol when my head pounded. I still had wicked Braxton Hicks contractions from about 28 weeks on — but that didn't stop me from enjoying a great Barenaked Ladies concert at seven and a half months pregnant, while gripping the front row seats at Massey Hall as each contraction hit me.

My parents, in-laws, and many friends couldn't understand how I could even consider such a thing.

"I'm worried," my mother said.

"Are you worried because I'm having a baby for another family, or would you be as worried if this baby was for me?" I asked.

"Heather, you're thirty-six years old. I'd be worried even if you were keeping this baby."

"Mom, think about it. Your mother had you when she was thirty-seven. I'm a year younger than she was." That seemed to mollify her.

My father-in-law just couldn't wrap his head around the idea at all. It took my four-year-old daughter to explain it to him one night at dinner.

"Grandpa, you know how sometimes two ladies want to have a baby, but they need a daddy to help them? Daddy helped Veronica and Carolyn. Well, sometimes two boys want to have a baby, but they need a mummy to help them. That's why Mummy is helping Michael and Ernst." With that, she shrugged and turned back to her plate of spaghetti.

When the baby kicked inside me — I let the boys know. When my belly button popped out — I let the boys know. I was the conduit through which the baby communicated to her parents. I never thought of her as my baby. Not for a second. Even though biologically, she was my offspring, I knew from the outset that she was *their* child, and I was in no way emotionally tied to her *in utero*. For me, it was really that simple a distinction — for another woman, it might not be. It's as if I had decided on a certain mindset and once that mindset was there, I was a "surrogate," not an expectant mother.

Michael and Ernst and David and I made a contract similar to the type of contract we made with Veronica and Carolyn. David's main concern was that my health and safety would come before the baby's when we were in the hospital. We also wanted to ensure that we would be in line for guardianship before the child went into the foster care system. After the birth of the baby, I would give up parental rights, and Ernst would then adopt the child as his own.

Right on time, at 40 weeks, I got to experience childbirth — the whole deal. I managed a VBAC (vaginal birth after caesarean), and got to endure lots and lots of oxytocin-enhanced pain. Oxytocin is the hormone that helps induce labour. In my case that basically meant that instead of having contractions three or five minutes apart, I had series after series of multiple contractions, one right after the other, with no time to practice any sort of helpful breathing to get through the pain. "I would like to discuss pain management now, please," I suggested pleasantly. Contrary to childbirth mythology, I remained polite to a fault. I partook of morphine and laughing gas before saying, "I would like an epidural now, please." The immediate relief that an epidural affords the woman in labour cannot be under-praised. I went from pain-filled weeping to intelligible conversation in the space of seconds. The epidural gave me a chance to rest before the final contractions morphed into determined pushing — resulting in the eventual birth of a beautiful baby girl: 22 inches, 9.36 pounds. As part of my birth plan, I had asked the midwife to make sure that Michael and Ernst saw the baby before I did. I got to watch as she was pulled from my body, cleaned off, and delivered into the hands of her fathers. I got to see the fathers weep and laugh and smile. It was one of the best and proudest moments of my life.

Michael and Ernst took their daughter back to their hotel a few hours after she was born. I stayed in hospital until my epidural wore off and then slept most of the day at my house.

Because I wasn't sure how I would react to the birth and postpartum, I told Michael and Ernst that I wanted to be able to define the parameters of our contact after the baby was born. I told them to let me call them when I was sure that I would be okay. I didn't want them to tell me when her belly button fell off; I didn't want to know if she had baby acne. They respected my decision and took her back to their hometown the day after she was born.

A few days later, I went out with David to Zellers, shuffling through the aisles to try to find nursing pads to soak up the milk leaking from my breasts. I saw infants in strollers and I wept. I didn't weep with the weight of emotional loss for this child; rather, I wept for the loss of attention from Michael and Ersnt. To be perfectly honest, I'd been central focus of an entire family for basically a year. After the birth, that family had a brand new baby to focus on. Not to mention the fact that they were respecting my wishes about not contacting me until I asked them to.

During my pregnancy, it was as if I had been beatified. Upon finding out that I was a surrogate, complete strangers looked at me with dewy-eyed adoration. "You're having the baby for another family? Oh, that's such a gift! That's so extraordinary! That's amazing!" And honestly, I wasn't offering false modesty when I said that it wasn't a big deal. It was not an extraordinary thing for me to do. Really. I am not a person who does extraordinary things. I'm a regular person. I do regular things. And yet, for the entire pregnancy, I had people telling me daily that I was an extraordinary person. It messes with your head. I had become Saint Heather, Patron Saint of Gay Fathers. I'm not saying that having a baby for another family wasn't work — the last 18 hours or so were pretty intense, to say the least — but I never would have had the baby if I had thought it was something truly extraordinary.

Imagine being a movie star and having people tell you all the time how wonderful you are. That's what it's like when you are carrying a baby for another family. The thing about having your own baby is that when you deliver said infant, the focus changes. Those who had focused on your stomach and offered you praise now shift their attention to the brand new baby and, hopefully, offer you support and gushing admiration for your newborn. But I didn't *have* a brand new baby upon whom people could shower their praise. All I had was a squooshy, bread-dough stomach and leaky breasts — no baby in sight. And did I mention that Michael and Ersnt were respecting my request about not contacting me?

I think things would have been easier if we didn't have fairly frequent and open communication with Veronica and Carolyn about their family. "Hey! Wait a second here!" I thought: "All David did was provide some lousy sperm, and he's getting all this love coming back to him. I carried a freakin' baby and went through some fairly intense pain, and I'm getting nothing!"

Of course, as David hesitantly pointed out, I had specifically asked Michael and Ernst not to contact me. (Did I mention that?) He also reminded me that, no matter how much we might want them to, men can't read minds. I realize now that I was living through some postpartum insanity. When I actually told Michael and Ernst how I felt, they made sure to keep me in the loop. Our friendship remains strong and grounded.

We recently enjoyed the first Ontario Family Day. All three families went to an indoor play gym. We cavorted through tubes, slid down slides, and jumped in ball pits. When we went for brunch, Rissa sat between her half-brother and half-sister. I marveled at the family tree that she gets to call her own.

These children whom we helped bring into the world will

know that we are their biological parents. When they are older, they may (or may not) choose to have closer relationships with us. What we, as a sperm donor and surrogate, are prepared to do, is allow them the freedom to travel the paths of their lives with their parents and be there if they want more from us. We do not know where the future may take us. Five years ago, I could never have imagined that we would have done what we have done. We have a very rich life and are blessed with a beautiful daughter of our own and have the privilege of knowing that through our help, two other children were born into loving families. *That* is an extraordinary and wonderful thing.

Not Playing by the Rules

By Damien Riggs

When my mother first heard that I was going to become a sperm donor to a lesbian couple, she asked to know more about "the ladies," in order that she could perhaps "know of her grandchild in the world."

I think I took her by surprise when I reminded her gently that she already had two grandchildren: the boys I foster with my now ex-partner. I also explained that, although I would be a donor to the "ladies," the three of us had no plans for me to be a "father" — or her a "grandmother" — to their children. Biology, I explained — again and again, over the next few months — did not necessarily equal kinship, equal family.

I am a parent. And I am a sperm donor. I am a gay man raising three boys, who came into our lives via foster care, with my former partner, who is now my co-parent and friend. For perhaps all these reasons, I have spent a lot of time thinking about what it means be part of a family. And for perhaps the same reasons, I am particularly critical of the assumption that a biological relationship must automatically equal family.

As it turns out, many people are equally critical of the particular family structure that my co-parent and I have created. Their criticisms and discomforts are often brought into sharp focus at the intersection of my roles as parents and donor. Friends and family, strangers and social workers, straight and gay, seek to position me in certain ways in relation to those roles, in ways that I have often experienced as problematic.

So, some background. More than six years ago, my then-partner and I decided that we would become foster carers. After a few false starts, our eldest child was placed with us. Some time after that, we separated, although we managed to negotiate an ongoing friendship and parenting relationship. Part of that relationship included polyamory, which asked us to reconsider how we engaged in intimate relationships. Through this lens, we could develop an understanding of what it means to love in ways that are less about propriety and more about respecting the multiple needs of people engaged in caring relations. For us, it was a way both to have an ongoing intimate and familial relationship with one another as parents that respected our shared past, while also welcoming new people into our lives. It also provides us with a way to understand the multiple caring relationships that the children we care for have: we can engage with their needs in relation to their birth families and our family without needing to prioritize one over the other.

Following the separation, our first child continued to see both my ex and me as his parents, and to see us engaged in loving and respectful relationships with one another and with other people. Many were puzzled by our ongoing commitment to each other as friends and parents: surely we were meant to dislike each other, refuse to parent together, and generally be antagonistic to one another? Further, we were told, surely we should no longer have an intimate relationship with one another — wasn't that having our cake and eating it too? These sorts of assumptions were often very challenging, particularly to us as gay men caring for a child of whom we are not legal guardians. We were very aware of the possibility that our "unconventional" relationship could land us in hot water, not solely with the people we dated, but also with the State, which acts as the legal guardian of all children placed in foster care in Australia. We both spent a considerable amount of time explaining to other people why our commitment to one another *was* very much family-focused; less about having our cake and eating it too, and more about negotiating a space in the world where we as a family and as individuals could grow through our relationship to one another, not despite it.

At about this time, I received an email from a friend who asked me to help find someone who would consider acting as a known sperm donor for some friends of hers — a lesbian couple. Once the discussions had been had and the contract signed, I began to tell a few select people about the arrangements.

Many of the reactions and emotions I encountered are typical to many men who donate sperm. These included the inappropriate sexualization of my life, where friends would make comments about masturbation. While I am a sexually active gay man, I was also brought up with a certain degree of prudery. The ways in which my sexuality was made visible through the process of masturbation and sperm donation made me immensely uncomfortable. To know that other people would know that I had been masturbating at particular times on particular days was, to say the least, challenging to me. Further, on some occasions, my duties as a parent overlapped with my responsibilities as a donor, and I had to collect sperm while the children were in the house — and then drive with them to drop it off. That unsettled me. How would people react? Would they still support my dual roles as donor and parent when the actions I undertook for the former could be seen as "distasteful" in relation to the latter? I worried that the already sometimes-tenuous nature of our family could be further threatened in light of potential judgments. The spectre of my homosexuality being read as pedophilia loomed.

In the face of my discomfort and anxieties, my co-parent very generously offered to "help out" in the process of collection. By so doing, he helped turn what felt like the unnecessary sexualization of myself as an individual into a shared action, a caring process between two parents in a family relationship.

Perhaps most disturbing, however, were the assumption by some friends and family that my role as a donor equated with my role as a father. Friends sought to claim a relationship to the child conceived through the donations I made. Rather sadly, such claims to kinship have not been made by these same people about the boys I care for, even though I know they care deeply about them and recognize our family as a family. One friend in particular — despite my repeated explanations of the agreement I have with the women and the fact that I am already a parent — repeatedly asked for photos of the child once born, and accorded herself the title of "auntie" in relation to that child. When I agreed to donate to the couple a second time, her default reaction was, "Oh, how wonderful that you'll be a Dad again!" When I challenged her behaviour and labeled it offensive, she toned it down a bit. I know, however, that she continues to see my decision as a wilful denial of the "fact" of biology, rather than an actual choice made via an informed understanding of what my role as a known sperm donor means in our particular arrangement.

Other gay men and some lesbians have referred to my presumed desire for "children of my own" (i.e. biological children), and I have been told off by gay men who appeared very invested in my investment — or lack thereof — in the child born from my donation: apparently I should want to see the child and to have a say in the child's life. For every time one person has referred to me as a sperm donor, 20 have referred to me as a "donor dad" — subtly reframing the terms I use to explain myself with ones that more closely suit their needs. Implicitly, these people are suggesting that I am somehow "irresponsible" in my actions as a sperm donor, and that I have somehow failed in my refusal to conflate the category "sperm donor" with that of "father."

What is my role in the life of the child conceived of my donation? Primarily, I am a friend to the child's mothers, and a signatory to a contract between us. As with my many other female friends with children, I enjoy seeing my friends, I enjoy seeing their happiness as parents, and it is always a pleasure to talk with other parents about the experiences of being a parent. When I see them, I don't feel the sense of propriety that it seems I am expected to feel, and this certainly hasn't changed since the birth of the child, despite the insistence of many that it would.

What I do feel, however, is the pressure of the eyes of others who know of my donor status, and who I feel misread my interactions with the women and their child. If I pick up or talk to a friend's child, no one bats an eyelid. If, however, I engage with the child conceived of the donation I made, I feel many eyes watching to see how I react. To me, this sense of "being watched" is a product of the assumption that biology should matter, and that somewhere, sometime, I will choose to let it matter.

Eventually, my mother came around to acknowledging my specific — and separate — roles as parent and as donor — roles that I had negotiated, roles of which she was not a part. It's not that I wasn't sympathetic to her viewpoint. When one becomes a foster parent it isn't necessarily the case that one is invited into a parenting relationship. Long-term foster parents in Australia do not attain many of the legal and social rights that birth parents often hold — a fact that places us in an unusual position within our families. We often don't experience the same "rites of conception" through which biological families begin: we typically don't have baby showers or naming ceremonies or nine months' worth of waiting for a baby. So our role as parents is one that is often tenuously negotiated, and sometimes feels under-recognized (though this is no doubt true for many parents). Grandparents of foster children may thus feel this same unusual relationship. My mother's vision of a child created in part through the use of my sperm as related to her was, perhaps, less about a denial of her relationship to our foster children and more her unexamined acceptance of dominant discourses of family and biology, discourses that provide little recognition of her relationship to the children I parent.

My co-parent and our children are often challenged, institutionally and interpersonally, by the norms of biology. This ranges from the mundane — having to fill out four separate arrival cards, rather than one "family" card at customs — to the more intrusive: people who question our commitment to the children as adults; friends or acquaintances who make remarks like, "You must secretly wish that you had children of your own." In the face of such challenges, it is perhaps understandable that we may appear defensive or wearisome. It would be a mistake, however, to read our reactions as paranoid or unjustified: the power of biology as an organizing principle is so ingrained that we are always already forced into a relationship to it, whether we challenge it or simply go about our own business as a family.

The two women have had their first child, and are now pregnant with their second, and within my own family we now have a third child. Again, this was a decision made between us all as a family (I want to care for a small child, as does my co-parent, and both of our children want another sibling to share our lives), and it was also a decision made between us as two adults in the context of an ongoing intimate relationship. Perhaps more than ever, we have faced questions and challenges: How will you cope with a two-year-old? Is your relationship really strong enough for this? Do you really need to do this? But perhaps more than ever we are equipped with the skills to manage those challenges and to clearly state our commitment both to one another as adults, and to honour our family and the children's commitment to us.

My previous critiques of biology are somewhat tempered now. I am still adamant that claims to biology can do damaging things to children, and I am still adamant that there are many ways to start a family. I am, however, more careful in my recognition of the ongoing salience of biology and its meaning to many people. I am also aware of the cultural location of my own understanding of biology as a white, middle-class gay man, and that meanings of biology for Indigenous communities, for example, may mean very different things when they are connected to sovereignty claims through the state's requirement in Australia to prove descent. Biology is thus, in my opinion, a set of meanings that are laden with both cultural and personal contexts. My relationship to biology, while still very much the same in relation to my own family and my role as a donor, is perhaps more nuanced in its recognition of the meanings that others will attribute to it, whether or not those meanings sometimes impinge upon or potentially overwrite my own.

While my co-parent and the two friends with whom I have entered into a known donor arrangement know that we are not playing by everyone else's rules, we are confident nonetheless that we are playing by our own rules and that those rules are at their very core concerned with the best interests of the children in our lives. In relation to the children born to my two friends, I take heed of sociologist Deb Dempsey's injunction for sperm donors to consider themselves "actors in the wings." It is up to the children to choose how they direct their lives, and to choose for themselves the people they wish to welcome into them. I trust in the mothers' judgments on how to talk to the children about their conception, and for the children to have the capacity to determine what they want to do with that information. The children may choose never to do anything with that information, and I will simply continue to be a friend of their mothers. They may choose to do something else with that information, and I am aware that this is a responsibility that I owe to them and to their mothers. While I challenge the legitimacy of biology as central to kinship in my own family, if biology (either as genetic information or kinship) comes to mean something to the children of my donation and their mothers, we will all discuss and consider the ramifications of that meaning.

My family's commitment to one another as people is what binds us together, not anyone else's beliefs about biology and kinship. Which is not to say that I wasn't concerned about how acting as a known sperm donor might affect our own family: as they grew older, would the children feel that donating undermined their relationship to me? Would the boys feel challenged or threatened if the children born of those donations chose to identify me as related to them? I came to realize that I cannot know the answers to these questions. What I can know, however, is that precisely because our family does not play by the rules, we will work through any feelings that arise for the boys in a way that respects their needs, while respecting the terms on which I agreed to act as a sperm donor. I trust in their capacity as people to trust in our relationship, and to know that my commitment to them is always primary. Between the five of us as a family, and working with those partners, friends, and family who share our lives, biology can be seen to matter on the terms that work best for us, and kinship can remain something that we negotiate in respectful and supportive ways. We don't play by the rules and according to the norms of biology. In fact, we actively attempt to refuse those norms, working instead to honour and validate the family that we have created.

Acknowledgments

I begin by acknowledging the sovereignty of the Kaurna people, upon whose land I live in Adelaide, South Australia. I would like to thank Greg, Nat, and Denise for ongoing conversations about the topics contained in this essay, and the many research participants I have spoken with who helped me to better understand my own experiences in a broader context. Finally, thanks must go to Gary, Jayden, and Liam for helping me to understand family in new ways, and to my parents Sharon and Robert and sister Lauren for continuing to support the family that we have created.

"He looks just like you"

BY RACHEL WARBURTON

Family resemblances have always been a fraught matter for me. I have two sisters. We look something like various other women in our family, but the story has always remained that I'm a Hilditch, my middle sister is a Warburton, and my youngest sister is a mix of my maternal and paternal sides. This was, and remains, a narrative that both connects and divides. It's not that the similarities aren't there — they are — it's just that the story is as painful as it is grounding. Being identified with one side of the family comes at the price of being distanced from the other. Feeling a connection always also means feeling a loss.

And so it is with the identification between our donor, Rob, and my sons. I love Rob. He's much more than a friend, something other than a brother. Ours is a relationship for which I have no name. He's kin, yet there is no biological connection between him and me. I once harboured the fantasy that my partner, Susan, and I would each carry one child and that the four of us would be connected in one genetic quadrangle. For several reasons though, Susan carried both our boys, but Rob's my family just the same.

Still, it jars when, as it all too often happens, on Facebook, casually between acquaintances, from random strangers in the park, someone insists that one or the other of my sons looks like Rob. It's not that the similarities between Rob and the boys aren't there — they may well be — but they are always open to interpretation, and interpretations are never neutral. The insistence on the primacy of biology takes many forms, but it invariably works to erase my relationship with my sons. Of course, no one claims this is what they mean; they would never mean to do that. It's just that the logic of biology is so compelling, so obvious, so inadequate.

Rob was, and remains, the perfect donor for us. He gets the significance of non-biological family. He had lots of his own long before we came along. Rob gets that although I share not one shred of DNA with my sons, they are mine. And here I need to resist the placating, "But of course, they are his too, in a way they aren't mine," because that is precisely the overdetermined cultural logic that I need to resist, and that Rob actually helps work to resist.

My responses to the exclamations that my sons look like Rob (or, more alarmingly, "their dad") vary from the gentle, "Really? I don't see it," to the more jovial but slightly confrontational, "Why do people keep saying that? Can't they see he looks like me?" Rob, too, attempts to intervene: "He's like his two moms spliced together," he'll say, or, even more accurately of one boy or the other, "Actually, he looks like himself." Each of these responses represents frustrated attempts to assert the boys' own growing senses of self, independent of biological determinism, or to secure my place in the family narrative. Sure, there are a million and one reasons why a queer girl might not want to insert herself into such a patriarchal, inherently heterosexist narrative in the first place. Yet when confronted repeatedly with the insistent erasure of my place in their lives, and with Rob's automatic inclusion by virtue of mere DNA, each resistance feels subversive.

And it's not just Rob whose place in the family narrative is secured first and foremost by biology. Susan too has had to learn that a moment's hesitation in response to the question, "Whose child is he?" can feel like a knife wound to me. The straight answer to that question, after all, secures her place at my expense. Together, we've had to learn to distinguish between people who ask out of genuine, supportive curiosity about how those of us in a two-uterus relationship decide who's to carry a child — that is, those who don't rely on biology for defining family membership — and those whose questioning implies discomfort and a need to reassert nuclear family boundaries. In the asking, it's a subtle distinction, but one with enormous implications for my place in the family.

Our family is bigger and more complex with more and varied

parenting roles than the biological identification of the boys permits. Rob's visits are cherished extended family times, and I wouldn't change them for the world. Still, his presence in our family is a bonus rather than a constant, and so when an older woman in our extended family describes Rob as a "very involved father," we all laugh. He lives in a different city, has never taken either child to the doctor or dentist, never been to a parent-teacher interview, changed so few diapers it's laughable, had no interrupted nights' sleep, has almost no idea what the boys like to eat, and invariably winds them up to the point they're in tears before bed. And then he goes away again, for weeks or even months at a time. Don't get me wrong, I'm not complaining. Rob didn't sign up for any of those parenting roles, and we didn't ask him to.

Susan and I love Rob's visits because they allow us to spend time with each other. He gives us a break. He too benefits from our arrangement. He gets to have children and spend two months traveling alone in South America. Okay, so I was more than a little jealous of that, but we've had more than one tantrum when Rob tries to buckle one of the boys into their car seats or hold them in a busy parking lot. They don't let him be a first-tier parent. I'm the one the boys come to when they're sad, sick, scared. If the price is that I don't get to travel right now, that's fine with me. I've done plenty of that before and there will be plenty of time later. Rob, as an extra(ordinary) parent, doesn't have to make that compromise. He actually isn't even given the option, since the boys don't choose him for support.

So, why do so many people feel compelled to insist on an immutable biological connection, visible in some (imagined) physical semblance, between Rob and the boys? Cultural anxiety at the heart of paternity, or plain old heterosexism? A little from column A, a little from column B? I can't decide.

The limitations of biological identification are also apparent in my own family of origin. Both my sisters have mixed-race children. My sister's eldest son, the eldest of all my mother's grandchildren, looks a lot like me, not surprising since I'm his aunt, and my sisters and I look like some of our aunts. If you hold his baby pictures and mine next to each other, the black-and-white of mine muting the differences in our skin colour, it's clear we're connected. Another, more recent, picture shows the two of us together; facing each other, our profiles and features are overwhelmingly similar. And yet, when I tell people he looks like me, some laugh, while others look away in discomfort. When I say that my other sister's daughter looks like her, I'm greeted with a similar disbelieving silence. People are keen to assert biological connections, but only in certain contexts, only if they fit predetermined cultural narratives of racial and familial certainty, a certainty that comes complete with its own set of connections and divisions.

I long to be identified with my sons and ache when I am not. I remember the first time someone told me my older son looked like me. He was about seven months old, and I'd taken him to a play group by myself, leaving Susan at home to get some work done. I loved that a random stranger saw a connection between us; I recounted the story often. A friend laughed and said, "It's amazing the power of convention." Although I got her point, I couldn't help thinking, "But he does look like me." And he does, sort of.

Both boys had blue eyes when they were born. Their eyes remained blue almost until their second birthdays. They were Susan's mother's eyes, sure, but they were mine, too. My love of their blue eyes, however, was never uncomplicated, was in fact somewhat complicit with precisely the same racial logic that denies my connection to my sisters' children. I am, after all, a walking pile of (culturally overvalued) recessive genes. When both boys' eyes turned to Susan's green, I was glad that they had her eyes, eyes I love and that I now get to see in three different faces. But I still wish that they had that, utterly random, marker of connection to me.

When folks choose anonymous donors, they choose race, height, eye colour, education. We know several couples who chose donors of the ethnicity of the non-biological parent so that the offspring would share some heritage with both moms. Part of the problem is, of course, the paucity of the categories available from sperm banks, but those categories are cultural imperatives that force our complicity with the hierarchies of size and pigmentation, that force our acceptance of the logic of biology. I'm not saying we were completely exempt from such complicity. We certainly weren't. But double-mom families with anonymous donors secure the place of the non-biological mother by reducing the donor to a set of predefined, disembodied characteristics. And I understand exactly why they might want to do this. The threat of invisibility is very real for me. But, for me at least, this threat is ameliorated by the benefits of the third, extra, occasional, unexpected parent.

When the three of us are with the kids together it makes perfect sense. Susan and I frequently comment on the benefits of a third adult and the limitations of the nuclear family, even a queer one. The "extra" adult means there's always someone who's free to cook dinner, someone who's free to distract children, and there's always a bit of down time for the various adults. Never the case when there's only two. (If this were a different essay, I'd insert a long meditation on my unfaltering admiration for and awe of single parents, but I digress.) The problems, for us, come when we leave the house, or venture out in subsections of our family.

When Susan and I had only one child, random strangers would demand to know "whose" child he was. Now that we have two, people assume one belongs to one woman, the other to the other. And it doesn't seem to matter which way around. Only once since our second son was born have strangers played the "Who's the mom?" game with us: when we both accompanied our older child to the hospital and left the younger one with his babysitter.

Sharing one child between the two of us unsettles people, but sharing two is reassuring, even in the absence of a paternal figure. On a recent airplane trip, Susan and I sat in separate seats across the aisle from each other, with one child apiece. Midway through the flight, we switched children. A fellow passenger commented approvingly that it was so nice of us to help with each other's kids. Women helping each other with childrearing is not such an uncommon event, after all. But my quiet, almost breathless, "They're both ours," silenced him, made him look away.

Then there are the moments we appear to be a happy, "normal" family, when Susan or I venture out with Rob and one or both boys.

Those times are by far the most discomfiting for me, because they assume a relationship between Susan and Rob, or even more bizarrely from my point of view, between me and Rob, that simply does not exist. And it's often even more bizarre for Rob to be interpellated into the position of patriarch.

By far, however, my favourite moments are when all three of us take both boys out into the world and people struggle to make us fit. When my mother named me after one of the matriarchs — Rachel, Leah's younger sister, Jacob's second wife, whose nieces and nephews were also her stepchildren; Rachel, the (temporarily) barren one who needed the help of her handmaid to fulfill her reproductive role — I'm sure she didn't imagine I'd follow her in stretching modern understandings of familial kinship beyond the (currently) intelligible. But there have to be more options than embracing the nuclear family, even extending it to include same-sex parents, or a return to some patriarchal idea of extended families. These yet-to-be-articulated options may require giving up the privileges associated with biological descent, but they may also forge new familial ties.

In order for me to be recognized as my sons' mother by Canadian law, Rob needs to cede his (automatic) right to the children. Then, I can adopt my own sons. I've resisted the legal adoption process and still resent it. The boys are mine, and I don't need a judge, and a not-insignificant legal bill, to tell me so. I resent that I have to provide legal documents and justifications for something that has been true all their lives, to submit to an administrative process that will make not one iota of difference to my sons' day-to-day reality. I resent that I'm supposed to feel grateful for Canada's (relatively) liberal definitions of family, and I am lucky to feel fairly certain that even if I don't adopt, my parental status would likely stand up in a Canadian court. It wasn't until a lawyer friend pointed out that my legal status in relation to my sons could be challenged in some emergency that I've finally seen my way to conceding to the legal process. So, Rob gives up his "rights" to allow for mine. This was always our agreement, and yet it rankles. His willingness to do so, to give up that which our culture so readily grants him in order to secure my place in our family signals not only his commitment to non-biological family but his unnameable relationship to me. It's a separation that connects, that both acquiesces to and troubles family definitions, that makes him my kin.

Mother of Invention

By Jenifer J. Firestone, with Hannah Sage Firestone

It is my daughter's fifteenth birthday and I am getting ready to go to her dads' house for her annual takeout dinner and sleepover party. Some of the guests will be the same girls who have shared her birthday since kindergarten. Others are joining the festivities from her middle and high school eras. As usual, I grab my camera, a bottle of celebratory champagne for the grown-ups, and a variety of photo albums including the one documenting her birth, for everyone's amusement and amazement. Her birthday always feels kind of sacred to me — an annual affirmation of an aspect of my life in which the creative risk I took actually worked out the way I had hoped it would.

In some ways, I had no choice. Five years before I had her, the seven-year love-of-my-life and I broke up, propelling me into the most arduous and frightening personal recovery endeavour I had ever faced. Having ventured with her into the baby-making process and then losing myself so badly in the break-up, I vowed never to have a child with a romantic partner. I just couldn't risk schlepping a child through the emotional upheaval I barely survived on my own. I wanted a co-parent whose primary relationship was with the child, not with me. S/he would never leave me because s/he was never with me in the first place.

At the same time, I knew I could never be a single parent. Financially, logistically, socially, and emotionally I knew I couldn't do it. As a community organizing-type social worker, money was always tight and a constant source of anxiety. I didn't want financial fear to become woven into the fabric of my child's life even if it saturated my own. I also knew that I would always have to work full-time and could not imagine the logistical, much less the energetic, feasibility of being there for my job and my child without substantial outside involvement from at least one other human being. Shared childcare and another source of income were crucial.

In addition to being a mother and social worker I wanted to be a lover and, if I was extremely lucky, find a partner. Furthermore, I needed time for myself and for my friends. An admired single lesbian mother friend of mine once said, "If you want to be a mother and a sexual person, you have to get your child out of the house." I knew that I wanted privacy and childfree time to explore the relational possibilities that are important to me, and to nurture my critical friendships. I also wanted solitude to attend to my writing and internal work. In addition to everything else involved in parenting. I didn't want to have to make special arrangements every time I wanted "grown-up time." I wanted it built into my situation.

Finally, and perhaps most importantly, I was and still am just too insecure to parent on my own. All my life I have struggled to manage anxiety and depression. I hate making decisions on my own. I didn't want to have to single-handedly obtain and process the relevant info about all 13 Cambridge elementary schools in order to determine which one to send her to. I didn't want to be solely responsible for figuring out which if any vaccinations to pursue, or when it would be safe for her to take the subway on her own. I don't always trust my own judgment, and I felt nervous and inexperienced with children. While there was nothing I could do about being single, I didn't want child-rearing to be yet another enormous responsibility I had to handle alone.

Despite the layers of fear and self-doubt, I had inklings of pieces of me that would be realized only through the unique intimacy of sharing them with a child I raised up in the world. As well, some part of me sensed that never knowing "my child" would be like never knowing a parent who dies before you're able to know her. I feared that I would grieve that incredibly significant, lost relationship. I didn't want to miss out on it simply because I was too afraid. To be a successful mother I needed another parent who could compensate for the myriad ways in which I was too apprehensive to parent on my own. I needed an arrangement that would honour my undeniable fear of and aversion to parental responsibility as well as my deep desire for a parent/child relationship.

As a lesbian who has always lived, worked with, and shared close and loving relationships with gay men, co-parenting with one was not out of my comfort zone. Coordinating the alternative-parenting program at a local LGBT community health centre offered the fringe benefit of meeting many gay men who were interested in being dads.

Robb was a co-worker I truly admired and enjoyed. He was handsome, funny, had tons of integrity, political leanings that indicated a shared worldview, judgment I generally trusted, and a clear interest in parenting. We weren't yet friends, however, and asking him to get together to talk with me about co-parenting was probably the most awkward and uncomfortable thing I have ever done. It was awkward for him as well, but he didn't say no. We got together several times to discuss my vision of equally shared parenting. While it was somewhat premature for him (being five years younger than me) he was interested.

At the time, he was dating Rick, and the two of them had decided to move in together. Clearly, if I was going to co-parent with Robb I would co-parent with Rick as well. And that scared me. Rick was and is a wonderful guy — with a master's degree in early childhood education! But the shared worldview wasn't there between us, and his lack of familiarity with lesbians and lefty politics disconcerted me. Even more daunting was being a single woman dealing with a male couple.

Seven years later, as I lay in bed on vacation with the daughter the three of us eventually had together, she asked about some of the circumstances by which we came to have her. She wanted to know why I was concerned about parenting with two men. I told her that as a single woman I was afraid that they would have more power than me. "Mommy, what's power?" she asked. She was too young to know about the historical oppression of women by men, much less the fact that the feminist movement had only scratched the surface of modern men's consciousness about the insidiousness of their male privilege. And, even today, the most progressive couples are clueless about the psychic and financial power differentials between coupled and single people.

Robb and Rick had their own concerns, including how to treat Rick's role as the non-biological and therefore non-legal parent. Our collective response was a painstaking, earnest, two-year discussion and writing process that resulted in a comprehensive, 35-page co-parenting agreement. Recognizing the multi-faceted complexity of this lifelong commitment that would govern Hannah's life as well as ours, we wanted to address every legal, medical, financial, social, and logistical eventuality of co-parenting that we, our three lawyers, and every friend and acquaintance with whom we talked could possibly anticipate. Between Rick's easygoing open-mindedness, my creativity, and Robb's tenacity and attention to detail we were able to clarify and articulate specific plans and expectations for our relationships with each other and our respective relationships with our future child. We recognized the possibility that any of us could have a change of heart, mind, or circumstance and committed to an alternative dispute resolution process for managing any such changes outside of a conventional court of law.

We were fortunate that issues that might have been problematic for us turned out not to be. I was glad that they (both non-practicing Catholics) were willing to allow me to raise our child to be Jewish. They were relieved that I, while Jewish, was vehemently opposed to circumcision. I was glad that they were willing to have the child take my last name. They were glad that I was willing to acknowledge and heavily document that this child would have three full-fledged, fully functional parents with full and equal rights and responsibilities despite the fact that the legal system did not allow for such an arrangement. I was happy to give them Christmas with Rick's family while she and I celebrate Thanksgiving with my family. I am proud of our agreement-writing process. The resulting document has served us incredibly well. We've had differences, but not conflicts. For the most part things have gone quite smoothly and exactly as we planned — except for one not-so-minor dilemma.

After Hannah was born, the guys slept in her room in my apartment so they could get up with her when she awakened during the night, change her diaper, and bring her to my room where I could nurse her. The plan was that after six weeks, the guys would move back to their house, and Hannah would begin alternating nights between our homes. Shortly thereafter, I would go back to work four days a week, and each of them would take paternity leave two days per week.

We had established an elaborate plan to assure that I could continue breastfeeding during this transition. Only eight days after delivery, still bleary and riddled with postpartum depression, exhaustion, and anxiety, I rented a super-duper, bi-manual electric breast pump and began stockpiling frozen baggies of breast milk for all the time Hannah would not be with me. Once a day when I was working, Robb or Rick would bring Hannah to me to nurse, and when she stayed at their house every other night I would go to her to nurse every third feeding. My La Leche League consultant was aghast. The La Leche League's expertise in breast-feeding and breast pumping is unparalleled, but their literature explicitly states that the role of the father during the first months is to facilitate the relationship between the mother and the child. Obviously, this philosophy wouldn't fly with my guys or with me, for that matter.

As the time approached for the baby to spend nights at the guys' house, however, my anxiety and depression went through the roof, despite our principles and planning. I loved breast-feeding, but who would have known that this tiny thing would still be nursing only five minutes at a time, three or four times a night? How could I wake myself up to pump so many times during the night to maintain the production she would need when she was with me? After sleeping for six weeks on the floor of my three-room apartment, the guys were more than ready to be in their house, parenting their baby with each other. I didn't want to deny them this or the plan we had made, but I wasn't ready, and we knew we were in trouble.

Maternal ambivalence is a major taboo in American society. Actually expressing that ambivalence and creating an entire parenting arrangement to accommodate it bordered on sacrilege. In the early nineties, many middle-aged lesbians with whom I worked desperately wanted to have children and would go to incredible lengths to have them. Many of these same peers were politely (and not so politely) skeptical — if not horrified — about the enormous risk I was taking by agreeing to share control of my child with men, and critical of my refusal to be a full-time mother. "How can you spend so much time away from her?" "Is that fair to her?" "Won't you miss her?" "How will you breast-feed?"

With intense emotional conflict on the horizon, the cacophony of doubts and anxieties emanating from my progressive community flooded into sharp consciousness. Maybe they were right. Maybe I couldn't have my cake and eat it, too. The dads and I, along with my girlfriend at the time, planned a meeting to discuss our dilemma. I imagined Rick clutching our agreement to muscle me away from reneging on our plan and keeping our baby all for myself. I was a barely functional, perpetually weepy, nervous breakdown with breast milk leaking uncontrollably through my already faded nursing shirt.

Fortunately, before that meeting took place, I attended the monthly gathering of my lesbian moms and babies group. We nine lesbians met throughout our pregnancies and continued to meet for several years after our babies were born. As coherently as I could in my distraught state I described the problem to my gaggle of moms. A short discussion ensued, in which soft-spoken Julie quietly suggested, "Why don't you spend the night at their house on the nights when they have her until you feel comfortable spending nights away from her?"

And that's exactly what we did. Disaster averted. The dads made up a bed for me in their living room. The first time she awakened I would pump while they gave her a bottle of breast milk. The second time I would nurse her and so on. After a short time she was waking up less frequently, and I was slightly more able to spend nights away from her. We settled into an elaborate but manageable schedule that allowed me to nurse every third feeding when she was with them, pumping in between. We even had a silent signal whereby they would leave their porch light off when they went to bed if she had not yet awakened for her late night feeding and turn it on if she had. Driving home with a friend or date at midnight, I could swing by their house, let myself in, and nurse her if the light was still off. I would turn it on when I left so they would know she had been fed. In general, I pumped like a maniac, and Hannah never went more than two feedings away from me. For me it was a labour of love and commitment to breast milk. For Robb and Rick it was a preference for breast milk and honouring something that was important to me.

After six months, we introduced solid foods. Two and a half years later, she and I (reluctantly) stopped nursing altogether. To celebrate, the guys brought me one of those "sweet 'n' nasty" titty cakes that said, "Thanks for a job well done." It was very sweet and very funny.

Ever since those first two months, Hannah has lived half-time with her dads and half-time with me. She spends Monday and Wednesday nights with me, Tuesday and Thursday nights with her dads, and every other weekend she alternates households. When she was younger, the parent with whom she awakened would take her to school, and the parent with whom she would go to sleep would pick her up from school (or swimming, or Hebrew school, or gymnastics, soccer, or dance). All four of us have appreciated the regularity and predictability of our schedule but have always been easy and flexible about changes and modifications that we all require from time to time.

We get together for a family meeting twice a month to work out scheduling, plan summers/vacations/family celebrations, review report cards ("a pleasure to have in class," don'tcha know), and make other decisions as needed. We total our "child-related expenses" quarterly, and share these based on a percentage of our respective incomes. Contrary to other people's predictions of "how complicated it must be," our scheduling, finances, decision-making, and logistics have been remarkably simple, accommodating, and uneventful.

The guys and I never went crazy trying to make everything absolutely consistent between the two houses. They didn't like gum chewing, and I was okay with it. So, she knew she could chew gum at my house and not at their house. They were able to get her to relinquish her beloved binky (pacifier) a good six months before I was able get her to release it wrenchingly to Jamaica Pond. In other words, mom and dads didn't agree on everything, so some things were one way at their house and a different way at mine, and she managed that fine.

Less smooth have been our emotional differences and dynamics. We knew from the outset that, emotionally speaking, we were like different species of human beings. I am the very emotional one, experiencing and exuding great joy and great sorrow, and functioning relatively well given the significant amount of emotional management required. They are much more even-keeled and matter-of-fact, without emotional muss and fuss. While still in the talking phase, I asked Robb how we would manage these differences. Characteristically, he responded, "I guess we just have to accept them." This good advice has been my mantra on many occasions, but it hasn't been easy.

I was one of the small percentage of women who experienced hyperemesis throughout pregnancy. In other words, I puked mercilessly for seven months, which further fueled my anxiety, because my baby was so "small for dates." In desperation, I resorted to anti-nausea medication that completely zapped my energy, increased my depression, and further exacerbated my anxiety: while I could now keep food down to provide nutrition to the baby, I was also feeding her these chemicals!

Emotionally and functionally it would have been helpful and comforting to me if Rick and Robb had offered to help with cleaning, shopping, meal prep, or laundry. At one point I did ask them to pack my lunch each day (all three of us are lunch-packers) since I needed to deal with food as little as possible. They could have said, "Sure. That would be a good way for us to help you through this nauseating part of the process." They didn't say no, but they didn't actually keep up the lunch packing after a few days. It was as though the co-parenting collaboration didn't really begin until the baby was outside of me. While she was inside of me she was my responsibility. My godsend of a girlfriend at the time was furious when, in the midst of all this, they took a class for new dads. She thought they needed a class in caring for the person who is carrying your baby. My inability to ask for what I wanted was my unhelpful contribution to the situation. The fact that we were not romantic partners or even close friends, that we didn't know each other very well, didn't live together, and had only planned the co-parenting but not the pre-parenting part of this project made for a problematic pregnancy and postpartum period.

In our daily lives, they smoothly share expenses, household, and child care responsibilities, while I tend to feel like I am just barely keeping up, struggling clumsily to get it all done on my own. It would be emotionally supportive and validating to me if they expressed acknowledgement of or appreciation for the fact that when our daughter is not with them, I am functionally a single mother — and that there are challenges to single parenting that coupled parents don't face, particularly when children are young. The emotional misconnection between us has been a hardship for me — painful at times. I have felt that my emotional struggles and life tribulations were either annoying or simply peculiar to these stable people in a stable couple. Ideally, it would have been better for me to co-parent with men who were more understanding and appreciative of my ways of being in the world. At the same time, I am enormously grateful that my daughter has had the beneficial influence of their ease and almost total absence of emotional and life turmoil, which I could never have provided on my own. They have been fabulous fathers to our daughter and flexible and accommodating to me in any number of ways.

My favourite part of this partnership has been reveling in Robb and Rick's great fun and humour, their unique perspectives, and the innumerable and amazing experiences, family, and friends they have brought to our daughter's life. My family of origin, my friends, and most importantly, my daughter are all crazy about them for many reasons.

The familial intimacy of having and raising a child together juxtaposed with our particular emotional distance and absence of romantic involvement has created a true relational hybrid. The trilateral association shakes out to be approximately 20% family, 20% business partners, 20% parenting partners, and 20% friends. The remaining 20% is an absence of emotional support, mutual admiration, affection or something like that, which has been the part I've missed the most.

It further complicates matters that we have no language to accurately represent these hybrid relationships. At my daughter's naming ceremony, just months after her birth, my father was earnest and good-natured when he asked how he should introduce my daughter's two fathers to the 100-plus friends and relatives who were assembled with the rabbi in my sister's backyard to witness our unusual family. "They're not my sons-in-law, are they?" Apologetically, I could only reply, "No dad, they're not your sons-in-law. You can say they are Hannah's dads. But in terms of who they are to you or to me, we just don't have the words."

This lack of words was best illustrated when, as I went through an excruciating miscarriage before my subsequent pregnancy with Hannah, the pre-op nurse assured me that "my husband was on the way." Superseding the physical pain, mental anguish, and anesthetic wooze was my infuriation at her assumption that he was my husband and my irrational determination to set the record straight. "He's not my husband!" I yelled. "He's a donor dad!" How ridiculous.

Not to mention how bizarre it was to have that donor/dad-to-be in the room while I was delusional with pain and medication and hemorrhaging from my vagina. Afterward, he confessed that he also felt weird being a part of that situation with me. On the other hand, it was bizarre that the other dad-to-be was at work and not witnessing the demise of what would have been his baby.

His emotional connection with Hannah has always been boundless, but, especially back then, he had no such connection with me.

Hannah did sense this. One time when she was three she asked one of the dads, "Why don't you love my mommy?" She also demanded to know why I kept going to all these single lesbian parties to which I did not bring her. I explained that I went to those parties so I could meet other single lesbians and perhaps meet one who could be my partner. I said that Daddy and Papa were partners and that I would like to have a partner, too. To which she replied, "Well, if you and Daddy and Papa moved in together, you would have two partners instead of one!" This most reasonable suggestion necessitated a brief but informative discussion about the different kinds of partnerships — Daddy's and Papa's was a romantic love partnership and theirs with me was a co-operative parenting partnership. How's that for creating language on the fly?

The highlight of my unique family experience was Hannah's Bat Mitzvah. In addition to being my only occasion to bring 227 family members and friends together, it was also the first time Hannah's three extended families met each other and my first encounter with Robb's dad. Rick's family and mine were always delighted with our familial creation and got together with us whenever possible. Robb's father had a much harder time accepting his gay son and family, as well as health problems that reinforced the geographic barrier between Nebraska and Massachusetts. But 13 years into the process, (Catholic) Grampa Johnson made the trip with several family members to stand with us queer parents and the other three grandparents, all in their eighties, to pass the Torah down to the child who had brought them all together. It was an awesome blessing and a stellar moment we will never forget. I have enormous gratitude and esteem for our extended families for their willingness to engage in our chosen practice of relational bushwhacking.

Regardless of the co-parenting experience for the dads and me, the obvious and most important question is, how has it been for the kid? What I can gather from her periodic commentary on the subject of her family life is that it has been a very good arrangement for her. Certainly there are times when the parent she is with is not the one she wants to be with. When she is on vacation for a week or more with one parental unit, she tends to miss the other. I remember occasional teary transitions from me to the dads when she was tiny. I felt sad for her to be sad, but I knew that they were geniuses at distraction and tenderness and that her sad feelings were momentary. As she got older, we talked about this "missing you" feeling, about how we all had that feeling at times and that while unpleasant, it was normal, manageable, passing, and not a sign of anything being wrong.

We have always welcomed opportunities to prepare Hannah for the countless instances in which she would have to explain her family to new and curious friends and acquaintances. When she was two or three she was playing on the popular neighbourhood playground next door to her dads' house. Local kids and parents were pretty familiar to each other, even if they had not been introduced. As Hannah bid farewell to "Daddy" Rick, who returned to the house, a little boy on the swing next to hers asked, "Who's that guy?" and "Where's he going?" I replied, "That's her dad. He lives in that house right there." To which he queried, understandably perplexed, "I thought that other guy was her dad." "He is her dad. She has two dads," I said matter-of-factly. He looked panic stricken and whispered furtively, "Does the other guy know?" That cracked me up. After I assured him that everything was copasetic he asked how she could have two dads. I explained that the two dads were partners who lived together in that house and that all three of us wanted to have a child and so we had Hannah. The explanation took less than 30 seconds, was age-appropriate for a six year old, and was handily absorbed by my ever-observant little one. I like to think that the normalcy with which we handle these situations makes them less onerous or charged for her than they might otherwise be.

Recently, Hannah wrote this about her own experience:

Today was the first day of the new semester at my school, when everyone gets new classes and teachers, and we all do the whole "getting to know you" thing over and over again. In my history class, our teacher asked us to write our names and four things about ourselves. Unlike many others in the class, I had no trouble coming up with numerous facts to put down, but the one that first came to mind was the fact that I have gay parents. This happens almost every time teachers ask us to share something about ourselves at the beginning of the class. Most of the time, I decide not to put that down. I figure, it is just my parents, they don't really need to know that, I mean, that won't affect my studentship, will it? But today in history I wrote it down, number four on my little slip of paper. I'm not sure exactly why I decided to include it this time. Maybe it was because I know Mr. Kwoba to be a political activist, and I knew he would find it interesting and want to show his support. I also realized that I *want* him to know that about me. I *want* to tell him that aspect of myself, not because it requires special treatment, not because I am worried about it or because I think it would somehow change my relationship with him, but because it is a part of who I am, and it makes me different.

I have lived every one of my 15 years as the proud and content daughter of three gay people. I have never once wished that my parents were not gay, or that there were not three of them, or that they had arranged their lives any differently than they have. So for any of those asking if it is fair to a child to raise them this way, or if they will come out okay, the answer is yes. I adore and admire all of my parents, and I think I have a better relationship with them than many of my friends have with their parents. But to all those who say that kids of LGBT people are just like children of straight parents and that we can live our lives just like everyone else, my answer is no. The fact that I know what "LGBT" stands for, for example, is proof that I am not just like any other kid. I learned at a young age that not everyone's family was like mine and that not everyone would understand my personal set-up. I have been explaining to other kids since the age of three that, yes, *both* of those guys were my dads, and no, neither one was my stepdad. When I hear someone say, "that's so gay," it hurts on a personal level, and when I hear about the fight for gay marriage on the radio or on TV, I know that it is not just politics, that they are talking about my family. I know I have had many unique experiences due to my status as a child of gay parents. I have a real perspective on diversity and on the importance of respect and tolerance. I feel extremely lucky and special because of that, but with the feeling of being special comes the feeling of being different. This feeling has not always been a good one, but through the work of my parents and some really good friends, I have been able to be truly comfortable with who I am and who my parents are. It is not a hindrance. In fact I wouldn't have it any other way.

Four things about myself? Well, I do gymnastics, I have two cats, I went to Africa when I was ten, and I have gay parents.

Of course, Hannah is not emotionally impervious to homophobia, which we know she experiences way more in her kid's world than we do in our adult world. However, having that homophobia acknowledged by her parents and living in a place where homophobia functions at a moderate rather than extreme level and where she has countless allies certainly lessens the burden of being "queer by association." Understanding homophobia from a very early age in the larger context of racism, anti-Semitism, and other oppressions seems to have enabled her to take it less personally, and feel less wounded and more empowered to work for justice in the world.

The benefits of full self-acceptance for any minority person cannot be underestimated. I am delighted that my unequivocal embrace of my gayness and my queer community made the possibility of finding gay dads and raising a child with them as natural and surprisingly easy as it has been. The parenting and co-parenting experience has surpassed anything I could have imagined, and we're only partway through the process! The extent to which we three have grown together as a parenting unit and been unique role models to our daughter has been deeply satisfying. Our family's sometimes process-heavy and often-comical style of thoughtful, democratic governance has provided a positive and useful example for her to live by. The extent to which I have grown and become more confident as a person and as a mother is a dream come true and is a direct result of this arrangement. To be this pleased with the parent I've turned out to be and this in love with the person my daughter has turned out to be is the most thrilling experience of my life.

The greatest blessing of our arrangement is the gift of time — time for self, for family and friends, for community, and for self-actualization. Robb's triathlons and political involvement, Rick's amazing house projects (both his own and those he does at other people's homes), and my writing and romantic life are examples of aspirations more easily realized because of the significant amount of child-free time our arrangement created for each of us. Self-actualization requires some amount of discretionary time and psychic space. The Christian Coalition-type folks would have us believe that raising children requires and should be afforded total self-sacrifice. My co-parenting experience has affirmed to me that this oppressive arrangement is simply not necessary. Further, I believe that adults have a responsibility to ourselves, our communities, and especially to our children to aspire to and live up to our highest potential. On some level I think that my daughter has been inspired and empowered by her parents' aspirations, efforts, and achievements.

Simply by being lesbian one forfeits any possibility of convention, reproductively speaking. Fortunately for me, this was not a problem. Conjuring up alternative models, custom designing a family arrangement, and part-time parenting have been incredibly liberating endeavours and have required an energizing use of my organizational and relational inclinations. Necessity has been the mother of many great inventions. I am relieved, overjoyed, and deeply moved that my family is one of those great inventions.

Learning to Talk

By Chloë Brushwood Rose

When Madeline was just five months old, and she and I were still securely floating about together in that strange, hormone-induced, gooey breastfeeding bubble, we ran into an acquaintance who is a friend of our sperm donor. She, another queer mom, took one look at the small creature in my arms and by way of introduction said, "Oh! Let me see Bob's daughter!"

The bubble burst. I had no idea how to respond. And in not responding, in not having the words to say something else about Madeline and Bob, I felt like I had been reduced to an incubator or some remarkably lifelike child-holding device.

It was a terrible surprise to me, although perhaps it shouldn't have been, that another queer woman and mother could so easily, and likely thoughtlessly, dismiss the work and experience of the two mothers standing in front of her and in its place reassert some archaic notion of fatherhood: "Who sired this child?" To my great dismay, this kind of reaction has turned out not to be archaic, but rather commonplace.

This experience of the force of other people's language was not my first, and nor has it been my last. Indeed, one of the things queer families seem to talk about most with each other is this very thing. "What do we call ourselves?" "What does your daughter call each of you?" "Have you spoken to her teachers?" "What did you say to the man at the gas station?" We cross out words on official forms and replace them with more accurate descriptors; we patiently explain our family configurations to customs officials, waiters, and strangers in grocery stores. But when Madeline was five months old, in some ways, the demands of this reality were still largely foreign to me. While I know what it means to live with my own story obscured, before my daughter was born I had never felt such responsibility for bearing the truth of another's story, nor had I felt the weight of those discourses of biology and motherhood — and with them, the demand for a father — settle over my body in quite the same way.

Early on in our experience as a family, Bob seemed better prepared than we did to deflect the words other people occasionally tossed at us. On a visit to Toronto during Madeline's infancy, we were out together at one of our favourite brunch spots. The waiter who served us most weekends — and who knew Elvira and me as Madeline's parents — turned to Bob as we were leaving and asked, "So, are you the dad?" Without missing a beat, Bob pointed at Elvira and replied, "No, she is." Bob's response was a huge relief to me. In those early days, we were still wondering what it would mean for us to have chosen him to help us conceive a child. We chose to ask Bob for his sperm because we love him and trust him and thought it would be important for our child to know about as many pieces of his or her life puzzle as possible — the sperm, the egg, the womb, the home. Plus, whether consciously or not, I think that both Elvira and I have felt the loneliness of having grown up in isolated families that didn't reach out to the world as much as they might have. Something in us was trying, I think, to extend the family we were beginning, to bring more people on board, to give our own child as large a sphere of influence as possible.

But we were still worried. Choosing a known donor also felt like a risk. We had both heard stories about sperm donors suddenly insisting on parental rights and preventing the non-biological mother from adopting. We knew that Bob didn't want to be a parent, and he knew that was our preference as well, but what if everything changed once the baby was born? What if he had an epiphany the first time he held her and suddenly insisted she was his daughter? I was nervous and anxious those first few months, and the constant stream of powerful hormones coursing through my blood profoundly heightened those emotions. When it came to feeling protective of my family — of Madeline and Elvira and our rights

204 — *And Baby Makes More*

to each other — I often felt like an animal, a tigress, the Incredible Hulk, Buffy the Vampire Slayer. Seriously. I was worried. And the protectiveness I felt, shared by many new mothers, often seemed to morph into defensiveness and anger.

In the face of other people's language and their inability to make room for the possibility of our family, I was pissed. I was furious at the thought of anyone, including Bob, referring to Madeline as "Bob's daughter." Bob had always been nothing but immensely respectful of our role as Madeline's parents, but what about when he wasn't with us? What did he call her then? What about his friends? We knew *they* all called her "Bob's daughter"… was this terminology being left uncorrected? In retrospect, these questions might seem mildly paranoid and somewhat overwrought. And yet the feelings were also absolutely well-placed, a response to the eyes that make me out for a straight woman whenever I am in public with my daughter, the words that erase my partner's role as her mother, and the strangers that ask over and over again about "the father." In that first year of Madeline's life, I was reminded over and over again that I had no language to tell our story, the story of our family, and that even when I could find the words they would often be misunderstood. I realized that parenting her as a queer woman was going to be another kind of crash-course in feminism. Ultimately, I tried to respect what I was feeling. And figure it out.

Let me be completely honest: I have at best an ambivalent relationship to the idea of fatherhood and a very troubled history with my own father. He was a bad to non-parent for the majority of my childhood, mostly absent and when present, incredibly destructive to all of those around him. And yet he was obsessed with the idea of "being a father," of having some biologically determined right to each of us — his wife and two daughters. Although unconventional in many ways, my father had an archaic sense of what "husband'" and "father" meant, one that he seemed sure determined his right to use and manipulate our bodies and destinies as he saw fit. As a young woman, it struck me as odd that a man who was so careless and hurtful toward me could actually claim the title of "father." Perhaps surprisingly, some part of me understood real fathers to be men who consistently participate in the loving care of their families. My "father" had not done that — he had not "fathered" me. Strangely, at 18 years old, I coped with this new realization by beginning to refer to my father as my "sperm donor."

Two decades later, I have come far enough to know that my relationship with my father is not properly captured by that term — for better, and mainly for worse, my father did live with me for a great deal of my childhood and was at times my primary parent, if a completely inadequate one. And yet, my study of our relationship, which began in my adolescence, both resonates with and perhaps is at the root of my own sense that, when it comes to families, biology shouldn't really mean anything. While part of me knows that it does — many other people certainly seem to think so — I can't shake my own powerful feeling that, in a world where biology doesn't prevent people from deeply wounding their children, biology shouldn't primarily determine the shape of families.

And sperm does not make a father. Perhaps more than any other, this is a belief that is hard for people to shake. In contrast to this belief, mothers are not primarily defined by their eggs and wombs, but by their caretaking, cooking, cleaning, nose- and ass-wiping, and so on. "Mothers" are those people who never get to leave. If they do, we are quick to take away the title and its meagre status. "Fathers," on the other hand, seem primarily defined by the sperm they deposit in women's bodies — or plastic cups — so that even when they leave, or were never present to begin with, they still get to call themselves "fathers." The language of mother and father, of hetero-normative family, negates the incredible commitment and intense emotional and physical work of parenting, done by both mothers and fathers (and others), not by producing a teaspoon (if you're lucky) of semen.

So, you might be wondering, why choose a known donor? Why give such importance to the biological act of conception by asking Bob to help? When we asked him if he might give us some sperm to help conceive a child, Bob was already part of our extended family. Perhaps in an ironic twist, as queers who have chosen an extended family of friends and loved ones, who in many ways make up for the deficiencies of our biological families, we asked a member of our chosen family to go "biological." Frankly, at the time, with no experience to draw on, it seemed like the simplest option, and in many ways it has been. And in other ways it has produced unexpected and complicated relations. While Bob is not Madeline's father, he and his partner are members of her family and an important part of her life. Yet, Bob's mom *is* Madeline's grandmother — in many ways she is as involved in Madeline's life as either my parents or my partner's. That is what makes her Madeline's grandmother — she has built a relationship with Madeline that is best described with that word. Our family is an ongoing experiment in making words and experiences line up, in finding new words, in learning how to talk.

Language has always been insufficient to describe queer experience. Sanctioned words for describing our intimate relations — "marriage" — have been kept from us and yet, when granted, some of those same words just don't seem to fit: "She's my wife? Really?" Even the words we invent — *butch, femme, queer* — get borrowed, stolen, used against us and, at times, come to feel too small — what does it mean to be a butch mother? A lesbian dad? And yet, we need words to live together, to speak and to hear each other, and to insist on the right to have our own stories. Becoming a queer parent — a dyke mom who was once a "femme daddy" — has reminded me of the importance of words, their weight and value, not just in describing my own experience but also in making a world that can tolerate the truth of my daughter's story.

And the questions that fueled my earlier anxieties about the force of other people's language, the questions that crystalized in my worries about what Bob was saying to people who refer to Madeline as his daughter, have not so much been answered as redirected. I am no longer interested in policing Bob's or anyone else's behaviour (except, at times, that of my now three year old). What *is* important to me is that each of the people in Madeline's family is committed to telling the truth of her family story: that she is the daughter of two lesbians, that our friend Bob helped us conceive her, that she has three grandmothers and two grandfathers, and so on. This is not so much because we are the people who know her truth best — she is that person — but more that we must each be committed to creating a world in which her story can be told and heard. This means inventing language and saying words that might confuse other people and make them uncomfortable. It might, at times, even put us in danger. But as the adult members of her family, who can and should stand up for her and make her world the best we can, we cannot afford to misrepresent Madeline's story for our own comfort, even when it's hard to say the words "sperm donor" to a complete stranger, or "lesbians" to the cashier at the drugstore, and even when it means refusing the safety and privilege of words like "mother" and "father."

My House on Stilts

By Cade Russo-Young

I remember watching my mom cut my sister's hair. Mom held up a book with a picture of a frog next to the corresponding word. Ry was supposed to read the word. I remember I could read it and wanted to, but Ry had to do it because she didn't know how to read yet. I remember she was squirming on the stool. Was that the time Mom nicked her ear with the scissors?

I remember other things that will mean nothing to you, but mean everything to me. Every family has those. They are what make each family unique. They are what make each family a family. They bind and unify. They give a secret language to a small group of people that creates a bond that spans years then decades then generations.

I don't remember the first time someone called me different. I was raised to never feel different. But I remember standing on a street corner between my moms and saying "Mom?" To whichever mom who turned to see what I needed, I would say, "No. The other mom." I needed to let people on the street, strangers who probably didn't even hear me, know that I have two moms. *See me? This little girl in New York City? I have two moms. I have two great moms.*

I remember the second grade. I remember Lizzie. "Kids with two moms can't do this. Everyone else can."

I remember in middle school, telling Briana, "It's not my fault." I was talking about my family. I was talking about my moms. I was exhausted after a fight. Again. Not a physical fight. We were only slightly more evolved than that. A fight that had to do with something gay. As a middle schooler, mentally exhausted, that was what I had left in me: "It's not my fault." I remember coming home and telling my moms. I remember the anger. "Don't you *ever* apologize for us. We are not a problem. We are not at fault." I remember knowing that they were right and hating myself.

I remember writing an article in high school lambasting my peers for their unrelenting use of the word "fag" as a means of insult. "We go to a school for the 'gifted' and this is all we can come up with? If you mean dumb, stupid, or lame then use those words. Do not equate 'gay' with that." I remember that was the article that they got the most letters about.

My mom told me a story that a camp counselor of mine told her. A kid asked me why my daddy never came to pick me up. "No daddy," I said. "Two mommies." He said in that moment he knew he would be okay. A teenager struggling with his own gay identity saw in me the strength and conviction of my family and knew he would be okay. And it was true. That was my family. No daddy. Two mommies. One sister. And me.

They are both my moms. And yes. I call them both Mom. I'm 28, and that's still the question I get asked the most. In my family there is no such thing as a "real" mom. Of course she's my "real" sister. What does that even mean? Would you ask these questions of an adopted child? I once told a therapist: "You have degrees on your wall from excellent schools. You're clearly not unintelligent. Just because you haven't encountered someone like me before doesn't give you permission to shut your brain off." She told me I had anger issues. I never saw her again.

I have donors. I don't have dads. Donors. Men who helped make us. I don't remember meeting them the first time. Or the second. I remember the third grade, walking to Brooklyn Plaza Park on the promenade with my class. I told my friend Thornton that he was coming to visit. How old are you in the second grade? Seven? Eight?

I remember matching pink and purple sweatshirts with our names on them in puffy letters. There were animals or flowers on them too. I think I got the purple one. I remember wearing them on the beach one time. I remember FAO Schwarz. There was a huge giraffe in a tower that played "It's a Small World" on repeat. Ry wanted a Corolle doll. I remember she got it. I remember watering his plants in his garden, but maybe I just think I do because there's a picture of that somewhere.

"So he's your dad?" No. He's my donor. My sperm donor. I remember running out of language at times. Fine. He's my dad. But so is he. She's my mom. And so is she. I remember that redefining language in a world that doesn't want it redefined was so challenging for a kid who needed it changed right away. I remember how that was used against me. Used against us. In a world that wants to place everything into boxes that can be wrapped up neat and tidy with nothing spilling over we burst onto the scene bright and colourful and unafraid. I didn't know enough to be afraid. Fear was never supposed to be a part of my life. But there's "supposed to" and then there's reality.

I have been speaking in hazy memories, and I need to tell you the facts now. First you should meet the family. My mothers: Robin and Russo. My sister: Ry. And me: Cade. Then there are the donors: Tom and Jack. I'll start from the beginning with all that "David Copperfield crap" that Holden doesn't want to get into, but I do. It was 1979 and my parents met, moved in together, and decided to have kids. They found a gay man who was willing to help lesbians start families: Jack. Russo was inseminated first because she was older. Pregnant on the first try. By May of 1980 I came roaring into the world. Overjoyed at my presence (and who wouldn't be?) they decided to have a second. It was time for Robin to try. The search for another gay man willing to help lesbians start families found them Tom. In November of 1981, I got myself the best sister anyone could ask for. I have already told you some memories. There are more. There are so many happy ones that I don't want to gloss over. There's riding horses in Delhi and swimming at Herring Cove Beach over the summers. Sleepovers, school plays, piano recitals, chicken pox (which may not seem like a good memory, but netted me some killer peanut butter and jelly sandwiches and hours of *Sesame Street* in my mommies' bed.) There's so much good I want to tell you, but I want to tell you about what happened too.

We had family policies. Do you have them too? No one is to know who is biologically related. We got asked that question quite frequently. "Whose is whose?" Who cares? It's not your business, and I can't tell you anyway. It's family policy. Family policies have extended to people other than just Ry and me and Moms. We gave Jack and Tom rules too. Or not so much rules as an outline of our family as we saw it. Of how it was to be. They had to treat us equally. They had to treat us as if they had no idea which child they had helped create. Biology was not to play a role in how they acted toward us. I think it must have been easier in the beginning when we were young. When we didn't have distinct personalities. I can't know. I can't remember.

I know that Jack got it. I know he understood. To annoying degrees at times. It coloured his gift giving. Those pink and purple sweatshirts were from him. I got something and Ry got the same thing, just in a different colour. He went out of his way to never show favouritism. It disallowed for individuality for fear of giving preferential treatment to one child over another, however inadvertently.

I think Tom initially got it. Sometimes I just have to hope he did. As we got older, it got harder and harder to hide. I was also a very perceptive child. I remember telling Moms, "He's favouring Ry." I remember not getting the toy I wanted at FAO Schwarz. I remember him making me feel like I was different. I remember him making me feel lesser than. Feel small. Feel bad. And knowing that there was nothing I could do about it was the worst part. I just had to try harder. I had to be better. Looking back it clearly wouldn't have helped anything. What was I trying harder at? What could I have been better at? He had made up his mind.

There were other protocols too. Tom and Jack were told explicitly that we were never going to meet their extended families. It was to be understood that they were a part of our family. We were not a part of theirs. All of this was decided before either of us came into the world.

"Why was it not written down?" I want to yell out loud sometimes. I scream to my mom in my head, "You were a lawyer!" I understand idealism, but maybe having children *is* a business transaction as much as it is an emotional commitment. Who could have known? It was 1979. They were mostly making up the rules as they went along.

You have to know my moms to understand where they were coming from. In March of 2009 they celebrated their 30th anniversary. They are more in love now than they have ever been. They raised us and never once apologized for their decision to bring children into this world. They ushered in a new wave of acceptance of queer families. They went to parent/teacher night and faced down the homophobes. They fought and fought and never backed down. They instilled in my sister and me a sense of self, a sense of pride, and an assuredness of undying love that we have carried with us through life. They are idealists through and through. They have always thought that people can be good. They trusted that when they chose these men to help them start their family, to start their new life, to start this new generation and be a part of a new movement in America, they could truly trust them. They *wanted* to make their new family on faith and trust. It was all so new. Waters untested. Lands uncharted. They were cartographers mapping new territory for those of us to come. Their idealism is something that I think both my sister and I have inherited. This belief that people are good and the world can change. The change that I have seen in my 28 years alone is enough to drive this home for me. This doesn't mean that everyone is good. This doesn't mean that everyone gets it.

There were warning signs. Looking back there always are. There was the favouritism. Then there was that trip. We went to go

see him. It was fun for us. Ry and I had never taken a flight by ourselves. We stayed with Chris. She was supposed to be family, too.
She was supposed to get it, too. I remember him inviting us to a
family reunion. I remember that crossing the line. We didn't know
it, but that crossed a line. I remember lots of yelling over the phone.
I remember a fight with Chris over the phone. I'd never seen Russo
so angry. And I'd seen her angry. Never like that. I remember closed
doors and whispering. I remember my parents being scared. I don't
remember my parents being scared like that before.

It was August. It was 1991. I was eleven. Ry was nine. I remember I was standing just in front of her, and we were looking at
Robin sitting on the futon couch in the guest room in our country
house. There were green gingham curtains that she made in that
room. There was a seafoam green metal desk in that room. I don't
remember if we still had the shag carpeting in that room. I remember the look on Robin's face and knowing something was wrong.
I don't remember her exact words. I think they were, "Tom is suing
us for paternity and visitation of Ry." I was holding a bottle of cran-
berry juice and I dropped it and dropped to my knees. I remember
thinking I was being dramatic, but I wasn't quite sure what the situation called for.

I remember we went back to the city right away. I remember
Moms went to meet with lawyers to see if they would take our
case. I remember we found Peter and Harriet. Peter Bienstock and
Harriet Cohen. I will never forget them. A part of me wishes I had
never met them. A part of me resents them. A part of me secretly
(I guess now not so secretly) hates them. But most of me loves
them down in a place I reserve for my fiercest love. The kind of
love that will never go away. The love I keep for family. The love
I keep for those loyal. Peter, Harriet, and Bonnie. I don't remember
Bonnie's last name now. Maybe it will come to me later. Bonnie
was my sister's law guardian. A law guardian is someone appointed
by the court to the child in the middle of the court case whose sole
job is to make sure that the interests of the child are protected. I
remember I wanted one too. I remember my parents saying how
lucky we were to get Peter and Harriet. How lucky that Tom hadn't

spoken to Peter and Harriet before we did.

Most people know their parents' voices on the phone automatically. Their siblings'. Maybe some extended family. I knew my lawyers' voices. An eleven-year-old who knows a lawyer's voice.

There are things I have forgotten over the years. But I do remember the fear. There was a long period of fear in our life. I don't know any other way to explain it. Fear. It stayed with us like a chill that won't go away no matter how many hot baths you take or how many pairs of socks you put on. Fear does different things to people. It made my mother stop eating. I remember my mother buying a pink suit. I remember it was very little. I remember long phone calls with Peter and Harriet reading briefs. Ry and I had to be very quiet, and we couldn't use the phone. I remember getting a second phone line that we didn't give out to anyone we didn't totally trust. Even much later in life, years after the case was over it was still a sign of trust if you gave someone line two. "Ooooh. You gave them line two. You're that far along in your relationship?" We don't have line two anymore. It was a strange sense of breaking with the past when we let it go. Ry and I had long since moved out of Moms' house, but it has always stood as a reminder of the case, at least for me.

I remember a court-appointed psychiatrist that Ry and I had to meet with. Myles Schneider. He had a yellow legal pad. I remember he had nose hair that flowed right into his mustache, which turned into his beard, which then met his sideburns and became his head of hair. He was like this huge mass of hair with a nose, cheeks, and eyes poking out and eyebrows like out-of-control caterpillars crawling around on his forehead. I remember him asking me questions. They were so strange to me. He asked me who my family was and I told him. Mom, Mom, Ry, me, the cat, and the dog. He asked if Tom was family and I tried to explain *how* he was family. I'm 12. They don't have a word for his place in my family, but Tom is family. He helped make my family. He helped make my sister. Yes, I know what a dad is. Dads do things like take you to skating practice at four a.m. or change your diapers. They have stories of exactly who you were as a little girl. They know your habits because they are around every day. They don't fly in once or twice a year and buy your love at FAO Schwarz. My friends have real dads. Tom isn't a dad. Myles, do you understand what I'm saying? I need you to get it. There is nothing more important in my world than your understanding me. Nothing. My family is four people. We are a house built on stilts. Four stilts. If you take one away our house will fall over. We are a chain linked together. If you take one away we will come undone. Ry is a stilt. Ry is a link. Tom is not. Tom has never been. Please tell me you understand. Give me a sign. I know what a parent is. I know what a dad is. I know what a mom is. I know what a sister is. I have a sister. I have two moms. I don't have a dad. Show me that a twelve-year-old has convinced you. Show me that though language might fail me at times the meaning behind my words has sunk in. You talk to the judge. You give a report to the judge who controls my fate. He ironically relies on your judgment.

And then something magical happened: he winked. He got it. A twelve-year-old girl with limited vocabulary but the truth to back her up had argued her own case and won. In my last session with him Myles winked, and in that moment I fell in love with winking.

There were small victories like that all through. And there were defeats. No matter what I tell you, never forget the umbrellas of fear that we individually carried with us like invisible accessories that burdened only us and only we could feel. The fear was with us all the time. It never left and permeated everything we did. I remember a similar sort of meeting with Bonnie (I still can't remember her last name). I remember it was the end of summer so it must have been August or September of 1992. I remember we were in Ry's room. Ry had a sleigh bed that Santa brought her one year. That was the year that we spent Christmas in the country, and Santa left us a note saying that there were so many children all over the world to give presents to that he didn't have a lot of presents for us that year. Looking back with the spectacles of my age I remember that was a hard year for us financially for a bunch of different reasons. I remember that being a wonderful Christmas and thinking of all the presents that Santa must have brought the children all over the world. But back to Bonnie and me. We were in my sister's room with the sleigh bed and the pink rug. It must have been late afternoon. I don't know exactly what happened. I don't remember it all. I remember I was telling her about my summer. I don't remember if I was sad or tired or just 12 and emotionally exhausted. I remember it started to get darker in the room. I remember I didn't turn the light on. It's not like it was pitch-black. It was just dusk. We came out of the room and Bonnie left and later Moms asked me how it went and I told them. I must have carried the same tired affect with me and their reaction was that of abject terror. It was then that I realized that it was one wrong word and Ry could be on a plane. Shipped off to Tom. Had I said the wrong thing? Was I not happy enough? Why hadn't I turned the lights on? Is Ry going away? If she does it's all my fault. I'm 12 and I have just lost the case for us. I remember feeling that it was all my fault. It was my fault because I wasn't happy enough and I didn't turn the lights on.

My whole life I have had to explain my family to everyone who didn't get it. I had to reiterate that Ry was my sister regardless of biological ties. I spent 11 years telling everyone that biology has nothing to do with the make-up of my family, and that biological relations mean nothing when it comes to love. Then suddenly Tom decided that the rules were to be changed. He decided that biology meant everything. If biology means everything and I'm not biologically related to him what does that mean for us? What does that make me? Where does that leave me?

I remember Mom coming home from court one day and describing a cross-examination that had gone well. Tom had shown a picture of Ry sitting on his lap while he was beaming down at her. I remember Mom showing me the pose. They then called his secretary to the stand and asked if the picture had been doctored in any way. She testified that she had taken the photo to be cropped.

She had cropped me out of it. Apparently I was sitting on the other knee. I was there. I was part of his life too. I don't remember the photos being taken. I don't remember sitting on his lap. But I did. I sat on his lap. I sat on his other knee. We were supposed to be equal. But I got cropped. He was cutting me out of his life.

I remember the story of a video that we had taken. I don't remember if it was at Stinson Beach or on Long Island, but there was a video. I don't remember the video being taken just as I don't remember the pictures being taken of us on his lap. I do remember that we had a copy of the video that we didn't turn over immediately. I remember Mom wanted to see what he had done to the video. I remember we wanted to see if he had changed it. He had. I remember them telling us what got cut out. You have to keep in mind that Tom was trying to make our family look like a lesbian bubble that had no contact with the outside world. He tried to paint us (or maybe just Ry) as children (or a child) who had no contact with men and who had no connection to anyone besides our moms. I remember the story being told to me as if it were funny. Triumphant even. And it was a win for our side even as it was a devastating loss for me. There is a moment in the video where someone mentions Philadelphia. I look up and with joy say, "Cookie lives in Philadelphia." Cookie is one of my parents' oldest friends and to this day is someone who I consider family more than any blood relative. I call her aunt. She calls me niece. Her children are my cousins. She gave me my first solid food. Our relationship and her relationship to my parents is one that again has no words in our unfortunately lacking language and can only be felt between us all. "Cookie lives in Philadelphia," never made it into his version of the tape. It was there. He wanted it erased. Maybe for other reasons, I can't know. But I got erased again. I got cut out some more.

These stories were told to me as snippets of how we called his bluff, of how he tried to manipulate who we were as a family and failed. To me they were nothing of the sort. How can I celebrate a victory knowing that the key to winning his case is forgetting me? How can I explain this to you so that you will understand? These men were not fathers, but they were family members. Family loves unconditionally. Forever. I am 11, 12, 13. Our victory moments come in the form of my being shown explicitly how conditional love is. Some of our small triumphs pull the curtain on him, both literally and figuratively, cutting me out of his life. The knowledge that his love was never real sunk in slowly but surely and never left. It is with me still. I was too young to tell anyone. I was too sure I could handle it. I got my period one night while Moms were out to dinner with Peter and Harriet. I had to call the restaurant and ask them to come home. I'm turning into a grown-up right here, right now, and therefore should be able to handle adult things like abandonment and crushing rejection. Right? So I put on a brave face. I never said how much I was hurting. I just thought about the photo until it burned a hole in my head. I just memorized, "Cookie lives in Philadelphia" so that to this day Pennsylvania will always remind me of her. I was 11, 12, 13 and I was conditionally unloved.

My donor had a hand in it too. When arguments began, when papers had just been filed, and lawyers had just been assembled, we knew that Jack, my donor, could be exponentially helpful to us in our fight to save our family. I turned 12 in May of 1992. For my birthday my parents said I should ask Jack to sign cross-adoption papers. This would grant Robin the right to cross-adopt me. Up until now we had never seen the need to legalize our relationships. We had always just understood them. But Robin and I are not biologically related, and under New York State law back then a child could not legally have more than two parents. We were asking him to give up his purely nominal legal rights so that Robin could legally be my second parent. I think it was April. Maybe May. I can't remember. I remember I was sitting on my parent's bed in the country so it must have been a weekend. I called him. I remember the phone call.

Jack: So your birthday's coming up.

Me: Yeah, I know.

Jack: Have you thought about what you want?

Me: Yeah, I have. (pause)

Jack: Well … what is it?

Me: I was really hoping that for my birthday you would sign cross-adoption papers so that Robin could adopt me. (long pause)

Jack: You want me to sign adoption papers?

Me: Yeah. I really do.

Jack: Okay. For your birthday present then.

I don't remember anything specific after that. I remember relief. I remember happiness. I remember feeling as if my act right there may have just won us the case before it even got started. If we could get Jack to show his support for our family we could show that Tom was just off on his own.

I don't remember how long it took but I remember the FedEx envelope it showed up in. I remember we thought they were the papers. I remember they weren't. They were cards. There was one addressed to me and one addressed to Moms. I don't remember my card. I don't remember if Moms let me read it. I remember he didn't sign the papers. I remember Mom telling me the gist of what he said in his cards was that he wanted to wait for the whole thing (meaning the case) to blow over. I remember the sinking rock in my stomach. I remember it because I still feel it even as I am writing this now. I remember the sense of betrayal, loss, abandonment, disappointment, and rage all mixed together to make a stone that started at the bottom of my ribcage and sank to my pelvis pulling with it all of my internal organs. He didn't want to take a side. He didn't want to get involved. He just wanted to remain neutral. In our fight there was no room to be non-partisan. Dante said, "The hottest places in hell are reserved for those who, in times of moral crisis, maintain their neutrality." You were with us or against us. We had no time for you if you had no willingness to help. Right now, winning this case is our whole world, and if you can't see how important this is then you have no place in our world.

Now that the case is finished, the whole thing did "blow over" eventually — much like a tornado blows through a Midwestern town. It leaves wreckage and destroys lives, but it does end. A month after the case "blew over," Jack died. To the end, though, he was typically Jack. He never showed my sister or me any favouritism. He traveled all over the world and went to Tibet on a number of occasions. On what he knew would be his last trip there he bought my sister and me both Tibetan rugs. The same size. The same shape just slightly different colours. Just like those sweatshirts.

Tom dropped the case in June of 1995. Jack died of AIDS that summer. In his will he left Ry and me equal amounts of his estate. Though I know he understood my family on the level that we always expected of him it didn't matter in the end. What good is understanding if you never speak it out loud? What good are principles if you never stand up for them? I never spoke to Jack after that conversation where I asked him to sign papers. He said yes. He told me he would give me a birthday present. In that last phone call I ever had with him he promised me. Then he couldn't. Or just didn't. Then he died.

The good in all of this pain is that there is a happy ending. I remember everything exactly. April 13, 1993. I was in my room. Robin was upstairs, and Ry was in the bathroom. Robin had driven us home from school, and Russo wasn't home from work yet. I was in my room. My blue room with its blue carpet and light blue drapes. Robin made those drapes, too. The phone rang, and I answered it. It was Russo. She asked if Mom was there and said, "Tell her to pick up the phone, too." I yelled to Mom that Mom was on the phone and she picked up. Russo asked where Ry was, and I told her she was still in the bathroom. So she just said it. "You guys. We won. We won the case." I remember I screamed. I remember I dropped the phone and ran into the bathroom and clumsily got down and hugged Ry. I remember laughing and crying and telling her we won. I remember it smelled in there and I didn't care. I remember I didn't even make fun of her. I remember going to find Mom. I remember the three of us jumping around in a circle. I remember Mom coming home. I remember lots of hugging. I remember lots of phone calls. I remember losing my umbrella. The umbrella of fear that we carried. I lost it. Or threw it out. It was gone. I remember such joy. I remember my moms crying and hugging. It was like it was sunny again. I remember hugging Ry with such security knowing she wouldn't go anywhere now. I remember jumping around again. Just the four of us in a circle like we still do sometimes when we get some really good news. That circle is my family and in those arms is love. We linked our arms and jumped for joy. We shrieked and shouted and held each other. We were four stilts holding up a house, untouched, intact.

My family made history that day. I don't know if you know it. I didn't really know the extent of it. I found out when the news stations wanted to interview us. I found out when the *New York Times* ran our story and the *Law Journal* and the *New Yorker* and everyone was talking about it. The first lesbians in history to win a court case against a donor. It didn't feel like history; it just felt like the best thing ever. It didn't feel like a civil rights issue; it felt like the judge just got it. It's not that we were busting down doors, we were just right and he was wrong. But we were the first and it was momentous — not just for us but for the world at large, so people did sit up and take notice. We put on a pretty face for the cameras and told them our story again and again and again. Just like we had told the judge and the law guardian and the court-appointed shrink. But this time it was different. We weren't fighting for Ry. We were explaining why we got to keep her!

The truth is that there were still two more years of litigation but that is all papers. Bad things happened. He appealed the decision. He won the appeal. We appealed that decision. And then in the summer of 1995 he dropped it. He just dropped it. He gave up all legal rights and said he wouldn't sue us anymore. Just like that. Four years of hell and it was ended in a memo. In one summer the case was over, Jack died, and I got adopted. For the second time, my family became a "first lesbians in history" family again. We were the first lesbians in the state of New York to cross-adopt. It was finally legal now. Jack was dead, Tom gave up all legal rights to Ry, so let the cross-adoption begin! I remember our lawyers jockeying over who got to be the lawyer on the cross-adoption papers. I think Bonnie won. Rabin! Bonnie Rabin. Thank god. That's been driving me crazy.

I remember the judge's office. It was the same judge that gave us the first decision. The judge who got our family. I never thought it would mean that much until I walked into the judge's chambers and watched him sign the papers. I legally have two moms now. I legally have a sister. I knew it before. It was just as true before. Nothing about our relationships has changed, but everything about the perception of them has. I remember we went out to eat to celebrate. I remember I was wearing a red dress with a white T-shirt underneath, and I think I was wearing jellies. I remember the picture we took outside of the restaurant by the Franklin Street stop on the 1/9 train. There was this huge sense of closure. There was nothing that they could do to us now, whoever the "they" were. I never really knew who they were, but I knew they'd gotten me before, and I knew they couldn't anymore.

This closure or sense of validation is something that can really only be matched by my parents' wedding. For their 25th anniversary my moms went to Canada and got married. I remember there was this great hotel with a loft bedroom area. I remember we went to Bloomingdale's to pick outfits for the wedding. The wedding itself was really wonderful. It was just the four of us. We went to Toronto. I remember I was a witness on their marriage certificate. To this day that's one of the things I am proudest to say I have done. I remember saying that this wouldn't change anything. It was just a sheet of paper. It was just pomp and circumstance. There was no reason for it. And then the judge started talking. I remember he said that they would never know cold again because they would always have the warmth of their love. I remember not being able to see anything because the second we walked into the room I started crying. And we were all crying because say what you will about little sheets of paper and ceremony and formalities, there is something to it. There is something to the validation and the finality of a witness and a legal procedure. I watched them holding hands and looking at each other as a man in black robes spoke. I thought of all that they had been through: Meeting, pregnancy, me, pregnancy, Ry, schools, piano recitals, dogs, school plays, cats, the case, lawyers, riding horses in Delhi, cancer, hair cuts on stools, lost jobs, summers swimming at Herring Cove Beach and Long Island, and here they were. Idealists to the end. Hand in hand in front of a judge with me and Ry because that's all they've ever wanted. Their family. And we were there. And it all came together on a little sheet of paper with a little pomp and circumstance. And no it didn't change anything about their relationship, but it changed something about how it was perceived and that can change everything.

I'm 28 now. By the time you read this I'll be 29. I've grown up. I'm a lesbian, too. And to all of you who might think that I'm just gay because my parents are gay I can tell you you're sorely mistaken. I'd tell you the story of how I came into my own dyke identity, but that's a tale for another time. I'm thinking of starting my own family soon. I know I want to be a mom. It's all I've ever wanted to be. And when I have kids, my wife and I are going to use known donors. You'd think I wouldn't. You'd think I'd be the last person on earth who would advocate known donors, but I'm not. I know I just told you this story of how I was hurt by a known donor, but in the end it's the not knowing that would have hurt more and somewhere my parents knew that. I will go forward, and I will try and correct some of the mistakes that my parents made, and I will make some of my own. But truth be told, I want to be moms like them. Idealists to the end creating a house built on stilts where each member is a stilt and the house is love. Creating a chain where each member is a link and the unbroken circle we form is love. I want to create a secret language with my family that will span years then decades. I want to carry with it some of the words

224 — And Baby Makes More

and syntax that I learned from my moms so that this language now will span generations. I want to recreate the family that I was raised in so that my children will know the love that I did. It is my way of saying to them, "I know no other way to show you how well you have taught me love than to love another as you have loved me. Thank you."

Conceiving

BY SARA LEVINE

"Let her always feel loved. Let her not be allergic to cats."

My girlfriend looked at me.

"What?" I said. "Can you imagine how hard it would be if she were allergic to cats? Let her love animals and nature and books like her mom, and languages and music like her dad." It was a prayer, really, but I didn't acknowledge it as such at that moment. We had some time to pass, we weren't really sure how much, while my dear friend, the sperm donor, produced his gift. I was incredulous that we had to leave the house while he did this.

I don't know what in the end made him say yes. Maybe it was just the repeated asking, the wearing down over time. Maybe it was the fact that I'd recently lost an ex-girlfriend to leukemia, someone I'd loved dearly, who was diagnosed the day after we'd split up. Maybe it was the fact that the frozen sperm I'd ordered from a California company was mostly dead when I examined it under the microscope at work.

"I paid hundreds of dollars for this stuff, and the best ones are spinning in circles," I told him.

"Really? That's crazy," he said.

"Yeah, I bet your sperm would be a lot more lively under the cover slip."

I'd asked only three men. One thought the world too horrible a place to bring children into. One wanted a child too much himself to do it. Then there was Eric. He never wanted children. A fact I still worry might be a result of my convincing him to work at a camp with me the summer following our sophomore year at college. How was I supposed to know he'd be assigned the eight-year-old boys?

The first day Eric handed over his gift, the glass jar was warmer in my hands than I'd expected. It had no odour.

Afterward, I didn't want to get up too fast. I worried that it would all just run down my leg, that our extensive planning, his visit, would all have been in vain. I called him in. "Come lie with me," I said. He did. He held me, and sang the theme song to *Sesame Street*.

My girlfriend, who could not be present that first time, was annoyed that I had gone ahead with the process without her.

"I can't believe you did it without me," she said.

"I'm ovulating today; you said you had to work," I'd explained. "What do you want me to do?" Our relationship was already unsteady at this point.

She wanted to be involved — not in the raising of the child that might spawn from this exercise: to this, she was not ready to commit — but in the actual conception. She wanted a pivotal, yet, uncomplicated role, which, for her, meant, inserting the syringe and pushing the plunger.

"I may let you push the plunger, but you aren't putting it in," I told her.

"Why not?"

"It might hurt."

When Eric learned that my girlfriend would be present for the second try, he had reservations.

"I can't do that," he said.

"What do you mean you can't do that?" I said. "It's not like we're going to be in the room with you, applauding or something."

I could tell by how he looked at me it wasn't a time for humour.

"You would be in the house. You would know what I was doing."

You're a man. I wanted to say. *We assume that's generally what you're doing when you have some free time.* But I didn't. I was suddenly gripped with this fear that he would retreat, that this dream, which finally seemed within my grasp, after years of negotiation, legal paperwork, medical tests and discussion, might turn tail and slip away, a white rabbit into a black hole.

"But, I was in the house yesterday," I managed to get out instead.

"But I know you," he said.

He sent us out for a walk. He'd call on my girlfriend's cellphone when it was safe for us to return. Before leaving, I placed a clean glass bottle that once held artichoke hearts on the night table and tossed some lesbian porn on the bed, whether to make him laugh or to be of use, I wasn't sure.

On the way to the park, I wanted to think about the baby, to talk about what I wanted for her.

"A healthy, happy baby. What else can you ask for?" she said, as we turned off Walden Street.

"How about smart and beautiful?" I said. "And kind. How about a girl?" I paused to let her join in, but she was silent. As we rounded the corner to the playground, I decided to continue my prayer aloud. The hell with her.

"Let her be sensitive enough to be compassionate, but not so much so that it limits her ability to be in the world. Let her dance like my grandmother. In fact, let her be as popular as my grandmother was, too."

It was January, and we saw no children at the playground. The two swings hung loose, and the ground was stiff and unyielding beneath our boots.

"Let us appreciate one another, bring joy to each other's lives."

"It isn't her job to make you happy."

"Can't you just humour me for a few minutes?"

It was cold enough to see my breath when I breathed out, I noticed. The trees were thin and still, waiting for their sap to rise so they could grow leaves again.

"How about a sense of humour?" my girlfriend said. "She should have a sense of humour."

I turned to her. Her shoulders were still squared in her blue and yellow Patagonia jacket, but her eyes were on the edge of teasing. I looked at her and, for a moment, felt that rush in what must be the uterus and travels downward. I wanted to pull off my glove and trace the line from her dangling silver earring down the edge of her jaw.

But instead, I said, "Let her have her father's sense of humour; let her get his jokes."

It was a dig, and I still feel bad about it, even today as I listen to my daughter's contagious laughter sweep through the house. Eric is one of the funniest people I know, but his subtle irony hovered just over my girlfriend's head. *Why is he such a nerd?* she often asked.

"May she never lose her curiosity," I said. "Or, her will to learn new things." Looking down, I noticed prints from children's shoes scattered in what must once have been mud. The trails were now frozen in place, thin, crunchy wafers of ice imbedded in each depression. I inserted the tip of my boot slowly into one to hear that almost metallic note as the ice gave way.

When the cellphone rang, my girlfriend handed it to me.

"Done?" I said.

"Yeah," he said.

We turned to walk back.

"Oh. One more thing." I said. "Blond hair and brown eyes."

"I can't believe you."

"What? I always wanted a kid like that. If you don't put out to the universe what you want, how can you expect to get it?"

We walked back in silence, for the moment having run out of anything to bicker about.

The third time was three days later, following a fight with my girlfriend. Eric was handing me tissues, trying to cheer me up. "I know," he said, "Let's do it one more time!"

"Do what?" I said. But I knew. "It's probably too late."

"Oh, come on. It'll be fun." And he leapt off the couch to retrieve the artichoke jar from the dishwasher. I laughed and wiped the snot off my face.

Alone in my room, I turned my thoughts away from the conflict with my girlfriend and towards the jar waiting for me on the night table. I stared at it, considering the absurd implausibility of the whole thing. The idea that what was in there might somehow join with what was in me to make a person. Yet, at the same time, knowing this to be true: in that jar were thousands of tiny cells, each one charting its path through the milky opalescence, each holding within itself a potential for what might yet be.

Contributor Bios

Torsten Bernhardt, Marcie Gibson, Erin Sandilands, Jake Szamosi, and **Andrea Zanin** are the proud queer family of the Spawn and the Spawnlet. When they're not engaged in group writing projects, they keep busy with such things as — respectively — museum manangement, divinity school, medical residency, feminist reception work, freelance writing and alternative sex education, pretending to be a pachycephalosaurus named Geezo, and bathing in amniotic fluid while awaiting birth. They live in Montreal (T), Kingston (M, E, S, and S), and Toronto (J and A), and spend as much time together as possible when geography and scheduling permit.

Mary Bowers lives in Chicago with her partner and two children. Her writing has appeared in *Inc.*, *Hip Mama*, *Word Riot*, and *Chicago Pride* magazine. She is currently working on a novel, *The Second Whack*, about a 14-year-old girl who tracks down her anonymous sperm donor. Mary's blog is at www.mmbchicago. blogspot.com.

Chloë Brushwood Rose is a writer and academic whose scholarly work has appeared in several publications, including *The Review of Education/Pedagogy/Cultural Studies*, *Gender and Education*, and *Changing English*. She is co-editor of the anthology *Brazen Femme: Queering Femininity* (Arsenal Pulp Press, 2002), which was short-listed for a Lambda Literary Award. Chloë lives with her partner and two children in Toronto where she works as a Professor in the Faculty of Education at York University. Find her at www.edu.yorku.ca/cbr.

Susan G. Cole is a writer, editor, and playwright. She is the author of two books on violence against women, *Pornography and the Sex Crisis* (Second Story Press, 1993) and *Power Surge* (Second Story Press, 1995), and the play *A Fertile Imagination*, a ground-breaking comedy about two lesbians trying to have a baby. She has also published numerous cultural commentaries in the pages of *NOW Magazine*, where she is Senior Entertainment Editor. She lives with her partner Leslie in Toronto; their daughter Molly is now 21 and studies at McGill.

Jenifer J. Firestone coordinated the Alternative Insemination Program at Fenway Community Health Center for seven years before founding Alternative Family Matters. For ten years AFM provided cutting edge education and counseling services to LGBT parents and organized supportive community programs for children of LGBT parents. She has been involved in the adoption or conception of over 1000 children to LGBT parents. The single lesbian mother of a 15-year-old daughter whom she co-parents with two gay men, Firestone has facillitated parenting arrangements between otherwise unrelated men and women. She is currently a hospice social worker in Chelsea, MA.

Diane Flacks is a writer/performer for theatre and television. She received an Emmy nomination for her writing on *Kids in The Hall*. She just completed a run of her hit solo show, *Bear With Me*, (adapted from her book), an excerpt of which was taped for a CBC comedy special and for a festival in New York. Her previous three solo shows, *Myth Me*, *By A Thread*, and *Random Acts* toured to LA, New York, and across Canada. She has written for publications including *The Globe and Mail* and *Today's Parent*, and is currently writing a bi-weekly featured column for *The Toronto Star*. www.dianeflacks.com

Susan Goldberg is a freelance writer and editor whose creative work has been featured on the CBC and in several publications, including *Bent on Writing: Contemporary Queer Tales* (Women's

Press, 2002), *Xtra!*, interfaithfamily.com, and *The Globe & Mail*. She is the recipient of the 2002 Editors' Association of Canada Tom Fairley Award. Susan teaches creative writing at Lakehead University, in Thunder Bay, Ontario, where she lives with her partner and their sons. She blogs at www.mamanongrata.com.

Rob W. Gray has published his poetry and prose in numerous journals, including *Malahat Review*, *ARC*, and *Douglas College Review*. His most recent produced short script, *alice & huck*, has screened at several film festivals, including The Big Easy Shorts Festival and the Beverley Hills Shorts Festival. His first collection of short stories, *Crisp*, is forthcoming from NeWest Press in early 2010. He is currently Professor of Film and Screenwriting at University of New Brunswick in Fredericton.

Rosi Greenberg is currently a senior at Brown University. She studies Anthropology and Arabic and facilitates creative expression workshops in a local school and prison. She has spent many months in Palestine learning Arabic and working with Palestinian artists and activists. Rosi is from Mount Airy, Philadelphia, where she was raised by her single mother and a beloved circle of family and friends. Her "intimacy constellation" includes seventeen (half-)siblings, a donor dad, a Dove, cousins, aunts, uncles, three grandparents, and several close family friends of various sorts. She thanks her family for contributing stories and advice to her piece.

Tobi Hill-Meyer is a genderqueer, trans dyke, colonized mestiza, transracially-inseminated queerspawn. She is a board co-chair of COLAGE, the only national youth driven network that connects people with an LGBTQ parent to a community of peers. She writes from Oregon, where she lives with her two partners. As a vociferous trans and sex-positivity activist, she is frequently diving into one project or another and can often be found volunteering on political and legislative campaigns. She blogs at www.bilerico.com and writes zines available at www.handbasketproductions.com.

Heather Jopling has performed Shakespeare as a clown, written four one-woman shows, several plays and three gay-positive children's books. She has been a traditional surrogate for a gay couple and her husband has been a sperm donor for a lesbian couple. She has a degree in theatre and is the proud parent of a beautiful daughter and two cats. To learn more about Heather's gay-positive children's titles please visit her publishing site: www.nicknamepress. com.

Sara Levine is a writer whose work has appeared or is forthcoming in *The Boston Globe, The Massachusetts Review, The Gay and Lesbian Review, Bayou Magazine,* and *Memoir (and).* Her essay, "What Hands Can Do," was nominated for a 2007 Pushcart Prize. She is a veterinarian and an educator, and currently teaches biology at Wheelock College. She lives in Cambridge, Massachusetts, with her daughter.

Capper Nichols lives in St. Paul and teaches at the University of Minnesota. He has a work in manuscript, *Alix14,* about his younger daughter's 14th year. Since the events described in "Donor Man," he has twice donated to another lesbian couple, close friends of the first; each woman had a child, boys now five and four. His daughter Naomi also gave birth to two boys, now five and three. The two sets of boys have been in daycare and pre-school together and regularly socialize outside of school; they are, in their words, best friends.

Damien Riggs is a lecturer in Social Work at Flinders University. He is the author of *Becoming Parent: Lesbians, Gay Men, and Family* (Post Pressed, 2007) and the Editor of the Australian Psychological Society's journal *Gay and Lesbian Issues and Psychology Review.* His research interests include parenting and family studies, critical race and whiteness studies, and reproductive health including sperm donation.

Cade Russo-Young was born in 1980 and grew up in Greenwich Village with her lesbian mothers and younger sister. After graduating from Smith College, she worked for *GO NYC Magazine* as a staff writer and went on to become the Nightlife Editor. She has worked in HIV prevention and education in New York, Boston, and San Francisco. Cade is currently living in Manhattan's Union Square with her girlfriend and her dog. She is working on her first novel tentatively titled *Across America On My Back*

Aaron Sachs is Assistant Professor of Media, Technologies, and Culture at St. Mary's College of California where he studies race, gender, sexuality, hip-hop, and the media. Born with the help of anonymous donor insemination, Aaron was raised by lesbian moms in Berkeley, CA. Aaron identifies as culturally and spiritually Jewish; as male, but not masculine; as straight, but queer; as a person of colour without a particular colour to belong to; and as an anti-racist white ally who isn't really white. Aaron also serves on the board of COLAGE, a national social justice movement of children, youth, and adults with one or more LGBTQ parent.

Annemarie Shrouder is a queer woman of colour. Born in Montreal, Annemarie is the mixed race child of immigrant parents. She currently lives in Toronto where she helps organizations create diverse and inclusive environments. Over the past eight years, Annemarie has written and performed poetry, and has written for and been the managing editor of two Toronto women's magazines: *Siren* and *Flirt!*. Writing is her first passion.

Bob Smith has appeared on *The Tonight Show* and had his own HBO special. He's the author of several books including *Openly Bob* (Rob Weisbach Books, 1997), which won a Lambda Literary Award. His first novel *Selfish and Perverse* (Carroll & Graf, 2007) was one of three nominees for the Edmund White Debut Fiction Award. His new novel, out in 2010, is the story of a 46-year-old gay man who time travels back to 1986 and teams up with himself to prevent their sister's suicide and stop George W. Bush from becoming President.

Shira Spector (www.shiraspector.com) is a visual artist, writer and illustrator with a BFA from Concordia University. Her artwork has been featured in a variety of publications, including *Lilith, Fireweed,* and *Canadian Women's Studies*, and on the cover of *In Recovery* (Vanderbilt University Press, 2004). Her writing has appeared in the anthologies *Confessions of the Other Mother* (Beacon Press, 2006) and *Who's Your Daddy?* (Sumach Press, 2009). Shira is a pro sex high femme infertile dyke drama queen and the co-mama of a brilliant six year old. She has recently received a Canada Council grant to write a graphic novel from this perspective.

Rachel Warburton teaches English literature and feminist and queer theories at Lakehead University in Thunder Bay, Ontario.

Dawn Whitwell was recently voted one of America's Funniest Lesbians by *Curve Magazine*. A regular on *The Jon Dore Television Show*, Dawn took her "subversive, slacker-next-door wit" on the road as a featured performer at the 2008 LA Comedy Festival and has also performed standup throughout the UK, including at the Edinburgh Festival. Dawn debuted her live show *Dirty Rotten Egg* to sold out audiences at 2008's We're Funny That Way Festival in Toronto.

Carrie Elizabeth Wildman was born in Mona Heights, Kingston, Jamaica to a Jamaican Mom and Trinidadian Father. The family of four kids and parents moved to Hamilton, Ontario when Carrie was an infant. Carrie survived a traumatic and isolated childhood by pulling pranks and cultivating her imagination. She admires the writings of Maya Angelou and Nikki Giovanni and is an avid fan of car racing. The most memorable moment in her life was the morning her son was born. Carrie, a true Aquarius, lives life with a purpose and resides in a small Ontario town on a farm with a few dogs and a beautiful, loving son.